ataleta
Loiero

The Kosovo Spec   stice in
nosovo?

Maria Stefania Cataleta
Chiara Loiero

The Kosovo Specialist Chambers The last resort for justice in Kosovo?

Avant-propos: Ornella Ferrajolo Preface: Robert Kolb

Postface: Fabián Raimondo; Renée de Geus

LAP LAMBERT Academic Publishing

Cover image: www.ingimage.com

Publisher:
LAP LAMBERT Academic Publishing
is a trademark of
International Book Market Service Ltd., member of OmniScriptum Publishing Group
17 Meldrum Street, Beau Bassin 71504, Mauritius
Printed at: see last page
ISBN: 978-620-3-46295-1

ORDINE
AVVOCATI
DI ROMA

The Kosovo Specialist Chambers

The last resort for justice in Kosovo?

By

Maria Stefania Cataleta

and

Chiara Loiero

Avant-propos

Ornella Ferrajolo

Preface

Robert Kolb

Postface

Fabián Raimondo

Renée de Geus

This book has received the permission to use the logo and the moral patronage by the Rome Bar Council due to its high scientific value and in light of its coherence with the values pursued by the Council.

TABLE OF CONTENTS

1. Two ways to face mass atrocities

2. The historical landscape and the role of the KLA in the Kosovo war

3 The path towards a new court

4. The European and international pressures

5. The mixed nature of the KSC

6. The *rationale* for a mixed tribunal

7. A new model of mixed tribunal

8. The transitional justice process in Kosovo

9. The necessity of public support

1. Essential features of the procedural system

2. Pre-Trial Phase: Investigations

3. Arrest and Detention

4. Indictment

5. Disclosure of Evidence by the Prosecutor

6. Dismissal of charges

7. Rules on Evidence

8. Trial judgement

9. Status of the acquitted person

10. The Ombudsperson

Post-face by Fabián Raimondo and Renée de Geus

Bibliography

ABBREVIATIONS

ACTWARN	**Activation Warning**
Ad hocs	**Tribunals *ad hoc***
CoE	**Council of Europe**
CoE Report	**Council of Europe Parliamentary Assembly Report**
ECCC	**Extraordinary Chambers in the Courts of Cambodia**
ECHR	**European Convention on Human Rights and Fundamental Freedoms**
EU	**European Union**
EULEX	**EU Rule of Law Mission in Kosovo**
EU High Representative	**High Representative of the EU for Foreign Affairs and Security Policy**
FRY	**Federal Republic of Yugoslavia**
ICC	**International Criminal Court**

ICCPR	**International Convention on Civil and Political Rights**
ICL	**International criminal law**
ICTY	**International Criminal Tribunal for the former Yugoslavia**
ICTR	**International Criminal Tribunal for Rwanda**
IMWG	**Inter-Ministerial Working Group Dealing with the Past and Reconciliation**
JKE	**Joint criminal enterprise**
KLA	**Kosovo Liberation Army**
KSC	**Kosovo specialist Chambers**
NATO	**North Atlantic Treaty Organization**
RPE	**Rules on Procedure and Evidence**
SCSL	**Special Court for Sierra Leone**
SITF	**Special Investigative Task Force**
SPRK	**Special Prosecution Office of the Republic of Kosovo**

STL	Special Tribunal for Lebanon
SP	Specialist Prosecutor
UCK	Ushtria Clirimtare e Kosovës
UDHR	Universal Declaration of Human Rights
UN	United Nations
UNMIK	UN Interim Administration Mission in Kosovo

The Kosovo Specialist Chambers

The last resort for justice in Kosovo?

Avant-propos

The subject of this book are the *Kosovo Specialist Chambers* (KSCs), a judicial body established in Kosovo in 2015, with the mandate of prosecuting international and trans border crimes committed there, during and after the 1998-99 armed conflict. The book is into two parts. In the first, written by Maria Stefania Cataleta, the founding instruments, the competencies, the applicable law and other essential features of the KSCs are investigated from the angle of international law, clarifying, at the same time, the historical and political environment that led to the creation of this court and determined some of its peculiarities. The second part, by Chiara Loiero, analytically explores the procedural framework of the KSCs, with appropriate references to concepts and rules of international and European criminal law and human rights law, notably the fair trial principle. Taken as a whole, the book offers, usefully, an early assessment on a still little known jurisdictional body, a further test bench for so-called internationalised tribunals, in the now wide and varied landscape of judicial mechanisms for prosecuting war crimes and crimes against humanity.

The Kosovo internal conflict of 1998-99 immediately evokes the atrocities, including ethnic cleansing, perpetrated against ethnic Albanian civilians by the authorities of the Federal Republic of Yugoslavia (FRY). These crimes were also aimed to crush the fighting of the Kosovo Liberation Army (KLA) against Serbs, and discourage demand for Kosovo's self-determination. The conflict ended following the Kosovo's air bombardments carried out by the NATO against FRY (*Determined Force*, March-June 1999). Crimes against the Albanian community are not, however, within the mandate of the KSCs, which concentrates on crimes committed by KLA against Serbs (mostly members of the RFY Army) and other opponents.

The jurisdiction of the KSCs does not therefore affect that of the International Criminal Tribunal for the former Yugoslavia (ICTY) established by the Security Council in 1993, which now rests on the UN Residual Mechanism succeeded to ICTY in 2010, for completion of the pending cases. Rather, KSCs should be seen as the continuation of transitional justice efforts made against KLA war criminals, initially, by the *United Nations Interim Administration in Kosovo* (UNMIK) and, subsequently, by the *European Union Mission on the Rule of Law in Kosovo* (EULEX). The case of the KSCs is therefore significant from the point of view, among other things, of the current fragmentation of criminal jurisdiction and consequent need for coordination among different courts. The functioning of the International Criminal Court (ICC) – whose Statute entered into force in 2002 – has proved not an obstacle, in fact, to the creation of specialised criminal tribunals, and all add of course to the competencies vested in the domestic courts. This makes cooperation issues no longer limited to the classic *aut dedere aut judicare* dilemma and possible conflicts of law.

Having roots in both the international and the Kosovo's legal orders, the KSCs fall, as already noted, in the category of so-called internationalised criminal tribunals, also named 'mixed' or 'hybrid'. Tribunals of this kind have some common features, while others vary depending on each founding treaty. The founding instruments of the KSCs include, internationally, an Exchange of Letters between Kosovo and the EU and, domestically, Kosovo's Constitution and ordinary law. The UN remained extraneous to this process. Decisive were, rather, recommendations from the Council of Europe and pressures from the EU, also aimed at facilitating the recognition by European countries of the independence of Kosovo, unilaterally proclaimed in 2008.

As discussed in the book, many of the statutory rules of the KSC, including on the appointment of judges, confirm that some regional elements are inherent to this body. A peculiarity the KSCs only share, up to now, with the *Extraordinary African Chambers in the Courts of Senegal* (EACs) created by the African Union without the involvement of the UN (which however represent, for other reasons, a *sui generis* example of a mixed criminal tribunal). According to some comments, the above circumstance could partly differentiate the EACs and the KSCs from other mixed tribunals – almost the totality – having their legal basis in an UN agreement with the competent State. It is early to say whether a process of partial regionalisation of international criminal justice has started, as the precedent of human rights courts might suggest.

In this scenario, the book here introduced traces a portrait in light and shadow of the KSCs, as a court with both strengths and weaknesses. Some of its peculiarities may pose questions or raise perplexity. It is true, on other hand, that the events linked with the armed conflict in the former Yugoslavia and Kosovo have often prompted reflection by jurists and sometimes questioned principles well established in the UN Charter or under general international law. This was the case for the establishment by the Security Council of the ICTY as an *ad hoc* and *ex post facto* tribunal, an unprecedented decision at the UN, the legitimacy of which under the Charter remains controversial. In turn, the NATO's 'humanitarian' intervention, carried out without the prior authorization of the Security Council, appeared to undermine the consolidated balance of competences in peace-enforcement between the UN and the regional organizations (Article 52 of the Charter). Finally, the self-proclaimed independence of Kosovo has raised the question of whether the scope of application of the self-determination principle should be extended to include peoples in situations other than the classical ones (colonialism, foreign occupation, apartheid) or recognise them, at least, a right to 'remedial-secession'. No substantive response is found in the advisory opinion issued by the International Court of Justice in 2010, on *Accordance with International Law of the Unilateral Declaration of Independence in Respect of Kosovo.*

The creation of the KSCs shows, once again, how complex are the factual and legal situations triggered by the conflict in Kosovo more than twenty years ago. As with the ICTY, what matters is whether the functioning of the new court will actually contribute to a fair and impartial administration of justice and strengthen non-impunity. Pending more KSCs jurisprudence, let me thank the Authors for their valuable work, which focuses our attention on one further experience in international criminal law.

Ornella Ferrajolo
Senior Researcher in International Law
National Research Council of Italy

Preface

While after World War II trials no international criminal tribunals could flourish, the 1990ties brought a breakthrough in this subject area of international law. The International Criminal Tribunal for the former Yugoslavia (ICTY) broke ground, the Rwandan Tribunal followed, then various hybrid experiences of tribunals situated somewhere in the spectrum between municipal and international law saw the light of day, heading eventually to the International Criminal Court. These criminal tribunals were an important part of the public order of modern international law. They were there to enforce – at late! – vital rules of international law in the areas of human rights, international humanitarian law and other branches of the same character. For this reason, these institutions were often funded generously: the ICTY (but not the ICTR!) had a budget roughly ten times bigger than the one of the International Court of Justice.

These tribunals had also their shortcomings. Contrary to the ICJ, they do not operate on the comfortable basis of a jurisdiction based on State consent. Thus, the concerned States may try to sabotage their action. Moreover, the jurisdiction of these criminal tribunals is related mainly to public crime: genocide, crimes against humanity, war crimes – the so-called atrocity crimes. These crimes are mainly committed by State agents and under the orders of the highest State authorities; or they are committed by armed groups which may seize the power within a State. If and when an international criminal tribunal indicts such persons, fierce resistance of the concerned State authorities is to be expected – at least so long as the indictees are still in power or enjoy State support. For tribunals necessitating the cooperation of States in order to collect the evidence and to be handed over the accused, this hostile or lukewarm attitude of a series of States, the ones directly concerned, the others political allies, is a major stumbling block.

The Kosovo Specialist Chambers are a hybrid tribunal: they function under Kosovar law but with international standards of law and personal staffing. The Chambers were created by the Kosovar Parliament on the pressure of Western States (in particular after various reports by D. Marty to the Council of Europe) and have their seat in The Hague. Their task is to prosecute atrocity crimes – namely war crimes – committed during the armed conflict with Serbia at the end of the 1990. These Chambers were thought to focus on crimes by the KLA / UCK; the deeds of the Serbs, on their part, were under the jurisdiction of the ICTY. Thus, KLA / UCK fighters' actions are investigated by the Chambers. One of the main problems this tribunal faces is that these fighters hold often important positions in contemporary Kosovo and display significant social influence. They try to sabotage the work of the tribunal by relentless intimidation of witnesses. With no witnesses ready to testify, a conviction becomes impossible, especially since after the many years passed, material evidence is most often lost. Justice is consequently stalemated, while peace is not necessarily furthered, since victims' frustration holds society under a malevolent sway.

This situation is illustrative of the main difficulty of these international criminal law experiences. They are caught in the antinomy between the exigencies of justice and the reality of a human race colored by nationalism. A universal value is stymied by particularistic thinking. It is a matter of experience that in all societies torn by violence – but indeed even in societies at large – persons are unable to think in a reciprocal and equal way under the polar star of the Kantian imperative. On the contrary, they view persons having committed even most heinous crimes under the lens of political considerations of a particularistic nature. Thus, a person is a national hero or a war criminal according to the side where a person stands. The same acts can for the same person be heroic or criminal according to whether they are done by friend or by foe. During the Bosnian war, the communities in the former Yugoslavia reasoned more than largely on such fault lines. Even today, a Bosnian student of mine in a discussion tried to excuse Erdogan's actions wherever he could, for the reason that he had helped Bosnia; if that student was a Kurd, he would have certainly reasoned to the opposite. There seems to be an inability of a great number of persons to attach to the acts and only to the acts, and to condemn them from whichever side they come when they are criminal.

International criminal tribunals have the merit to fight against such deleterious ideologies. They try to instill some portions of Kantian thinking: justice whether friend or foe. If only for that service, they cannot be valued highly enough. However, to be able to appreciate the work of such tribunals, it is necessary to make them better known by the greater public. Any publication in the subject area is an attempt at valuable public information and perhaps sometimes even education. Thus, we must be grateful to Ms. Cataleta and Loiero to have painstakingly and with talent analyzed the Kosovo Specialized Chambers, to have told us what they are and how they work, to have discussed the legal but also the more general issues they raise. To the first part, which deals with general issues, responds the second part analyzing in more detail the procedure of these Chambers. The work is concise in result, which will greatly increase its readability. If there is some literature on these Chambers, there is not much such literature. Thus, the present contribution significantly contributes to an increased knowledge on this important subject matter.

Robert Kolb
Professor of International Law
University of Geneva

Introduction

The Kosovo Specialist Chambers (hereinafter 'KSC' or 'Court'), a judicial body with a temporary duration, were promoted by the European Union (hereinafter 'EU') with ambitious expectations, as an instrument to fight the impunity, ensuring justice for victims, promoting state building, national reconciliation and peace in the whole region. Ultimately, it should be an institution capable to facilitate the Kosovo EU membership. The UN did not play any role in its establishment.[1]

The idea to create a new court was born when, in 2011, the Council of Europe (hereinafter 'CoE') published the 'Marty Report', that denounced the commission, by the KLA (hereinafter 'KLA', known also as 'UCK'), of crimes against humanity and war crimes committed against Serbians and Albanians collaborators before, during and after the North Atlantic Treaty Organization's (hereinafter 'NATO') intervention in Kosovo in 1999.[2]The armed conflict in Kosovo caused the massive displacement of the civilian population and the establishment of the United Nations Interim Administration Mission in Kosovo (hereinafter 'UNMIK').[3]

---

1   Gazeta Express, 'Jacobson: Should Kosovo fail, Special Court will be created by the UN', 3 June 2015, available at http://www.gazetaexpress.com/en/news/jacobson-should-kosovo-fail-special-court-will-be-created-by-the-un-105330/ (accessed June 4,2020).

2   Council of Europe Committee on Legal Affairs and Human Rights, 'Inhuman Treatment of People and Illicit Trafficking of Human Organs in Kosovo', Report No. 12462, 7 January 2011, http://assembly.coe.int/nw/xml/XRef/Xref-XML2HTML-en.asp?fileid=12608&lang=en (accessed May 22, 2020).

3   *See* Mertus Julie, "Reconsidering the Legality of Humanitarian Intervention: Lessons from Kosovo", in *William & Mary Law Review* 41, 2000, at 1743 ss.; *See also* Heir Aidan, "NATO's 'Humanitarian Intervention' in Kosovo: Legal Precedent or Aberration?", in *Journal of Human Rights* 8, 2009, at 245 et seq.

The crimes were reported in the Council of Europe Parliamentary Assembly Report Doc 12462 of 7 January 2011 (hereinafter 'CoE Report') and were the subject of criminal investigation by the Special Investigative Task Force (hereinafter 'SITF')[4] of the EU Rule of Law Mission in Kosovo (hereinafter 'EULEX')[5] Special Prosecution Office of the Republic of Kosovo (hereinafter 'SPRK').[6] In order to permit the creation of the KSC, on 3 August 2015, the Assembly of Kosovo changed the Constitution and in two extraordinary sessions adopted the Law on the Specialist Chambers and the Specialist Prosecutor's Office (hereinafter 'the Law').

The KSC are a Kosovar Court with international characteristics, typical of mixed tribunals (also 'internazionalized' or 'hybrid'). There is a considerable debate in doctrine on the particular nature of such Court, that would posses a marked prevailing international character, given to the presence of only international judges and personnel, justified as necessary to ensure the Court's impartiality and immunity from intimidation and interferences.[7] The doctrine, in relation to this Court, maintains that it reflects a process of "regionalization" of international criminal justice.[8]

---

4   The SITF derived its legality from the European Union Council Decision establishing the EULEX Kosovo and furthermore with the following agreement between the Republic of Kosovo and the EU, on 4 September 2008, it kept a special status within the Kosovo's prosecutorial system outside the authority of Kosovo. This special status was confirmed by Law No. 04/L-148, Art. 1, para 2 (a).

5   The EULEX was established in 2008 within the European Union mission in the area of European Security and Defence Policy with the mandate to exercise functions in Kosovo's legal and judicial system following Kosovo's declaration of independence in 2008.

6   Law No. 05/L-053 on Specialist Chambers and Specialist Prosecutor's Office, Art. 1 (2), available at : http://gzk.rks-gov.net (accessed May 11, 2020).

7   See, e.g. Muharremi Robert, "The Kosovo Specialist Chambers and Specialist Prosecutor's Office", in *Max-Plank-Institut für ausländisches öffendisches Recht und Völkerrecht*, 2016, at 968 et seq.

8   See Cimiotta Emanuele, "The Specialist Chambers and the Specialist Prosecutor's Office in Kosovo", in *Journal of International Criminal Justice,* 2016, at 54.

The mixed feature of this jurisdiction should feed a sense of ownership and legitimacy at local level, approaching the population to the judicial proceedings against the mass atrocities that have bathed in blood the country in the late 1990s, when Kosovo was a province of Serbia within the former Federal Republic of Yugoslavia (hereinafter 'FRY'). In fact, one of the most important mission pursued by international criminal justice, particularly the hybrid one, is to produce proximity with the local population and gain its support.[9] The proximity with the local population, realized mainly through the Outreach Program, is a substrate for legitimacy and ownership of a mixed tribunal in the national perception. However, today the KSC are target of criticisms by the local population as well as by political leaders and are object of debate by some scholars. Much criticism relate the lack of legitimacy and local ownership of the KSC, two above mentioned crucial elements for such hybrid mechanisms typical of transitional justice.

According to this critical literature the Court was not created in response to domestic pressure within Kosovo, but thanks to external pressure; furthermore, neither the Court's legitimacy has improved since its establishment nor its proceedings could receive public support in the future, in order to facilitate societal changes like expected by its external supporters, principally European Union and the CoE. On the other hand, according to such supporters, the Court should not only establish justice, but in the meantime it should promote reconciliation between Albanians and Serbs, facilitate the progress and stability of the Kosovar society and lastly, make the country close to the international community. On the opposite, the hostile societal and political context in the country foretells that the Court will

---

9   *See generally* Clark Janine Natalya, "International War Crimes Tribunals and the Challenge of Outreach", in *International Criminal Law Review*, 2009, at 99.

produce adverse effects, sharping inter-ethnic clutches, undermining stability in Kosovo and in the whole region, threating the normalization of the relations between Kosovars and Serbs.

In particular, the publication of the 'Marty Report' was negatively received among ethnic Albanians and coincided with the victory of KLA-affiliated parties in both national and local elections. In fact, they are the main object of the investigations of the Court and from that time, they contest any allegation that is interpreted as Serbian- and Russian-backed attempts to involve the KLA in international crimes. The aim pursued would be the reversal of Serb historical responsibilities for the Kosovo past conflict with the ultimate intention to undermine the recognition of Kosovo's independence. Furthermore, according to the sceptical opinions, today the Court would be perceived as distant, not only physically (being located in The Hague) from the Kosovo control and in addiction, it would feed particularly the hostility within the Kosovo Albanian group, who supports the KLA.[10] According to the domestic contestations, the KSC would discriminate against Kosovar Albanian guerrillas, whose ranks included President Hashim Thaçi; It would have been created by force and not voluntarily by Kosovo's population and politicians. Lastly, it would be a political body.

Part I addresses these arguments. Indeed, to these objections it is possible to reply that the Court is based on Kosovo's Constitution because the same Kosovo Assembly voted in favour of its creation, in August 2015, after some failed attempts, in order to investigate and prosecute serious international and transnational crimes allegedly committed by the KLA between January 1,

---

10   *See* Heir Aidan, "Lessons Learned? The Kosovo Specialist Chambers' Lack Local Legitimacy and Its Implications", in *Human Rights Review,* 2019, at 267 et seq.

4

1998 and December 31, 2000. Thus, the Kosovo Assembly voted expressly for it. One can observe that the same criticisms have involved almost all hybrid tribunals and courts on the base of similar arguments. This already happened for its predecessor, the International Criminal Tribunal for the former Yugoslavia (hereinafter 'ICTY'), established with a Security Council resolution and largely judged as illegitimate; but other mixed jurisdictions have raised analogue sense of refusal, such as the Special Tribunal for Lebanon (hereinafter 'STL'), established as well with a Security Council resolution due to the immobility of the country, whose government had in the first time explicitly demanded, and after denied, the international intervention.

It seems that the same destiny unites all international/mixed jurisdictions, that, if on one hand, satisfy some demands, on the other hand, discontent because of the double and mixed, sometimes "divergent" nature of them. It is obvious that the nature of a mixed tribunal means that two or more aspects of it are often divergent or maybe antithetical, for instance the international and national nature. An hybrid tribunal can easily satisfy the local demand for justice thanks to its national features, whereas it can satisfy the international claims through the international aspects of itself. Not always these two so different, sometimes opposite parts of the same organ can reconcile, it is a difficult harmony to maintain, specially in the public opinion not always ready to these anomalous experiments. Sometime, like in this case, the national aspects of the Court are not sufficient to obtain the domestic consensus. This Court became fully operational in 2017 and immediately, some Albanian's politicians tried to revoke it in the Kosovo Assembly. On the contrary, it was welcome by the international community, *"it is a sign of responsibility and determination to establish the truth and make decisions compatible with Kosovo's European path"*, said the EU Foreign Affairs and Security Policy chief (hereinafter 'EU High Representative'), Federica Mogherini.[11]

These kinds of tribunals and courts express what we call "transitional justice", a kind of justice entitled to face with past large-scale abuses, assure conflict prevention and achieve reconciliation. It is a justice difficult to enact and with complex results, that one can appreciate sometimes only after many years, when the population affected forgets the angry and becomes capable to critically analyse certain dramatic events of the history of the country. Despite the criticisms, the first author believes that the process of establishment and the particular morphology of the KSC are in favour of its full legitimacy even if it lacks ownership from a part of the national population. This is the assumption that will be sustained in the **First Part** of the book, after a preliminary *excursus* on the historical premises that conducted to the creation of the KSC.

Furthermore, in **Part II**, this contribution will address the legal framework governing this recently established hybrid institution, which with its establishment becomes an additional, contributing part of the system of international criminal law that has been developing since the ICTY began its work in 1995. In particular, **Part II** starts from two premises. First, that despite the high expectations that usually follows their establishment,

---

11   *See, e.g.* Collaku Petrit/Rustic Marija, 'Kosovo Praised for Approving New War Crimes Court', *Balkan   Transitional   Justice,*   4th   August   2015, http://www.balkaninsight.com/en/article/kosovo-praised-for-establishment-of-the-special-court-08-04-2015- (accessed May 21, 2020); EU External Action, 'Statement by High Representative/Vice President Federica Mogherini after adoption by the Kosovo Assembly of the Law on Specialist Chambers and Specialist Prosecutor's Office, 3rd August 2015, https://eeas.europa.eu/headquarters/headquarters-homepage/3230/node/3230_nl (accessed May 22, 2020).

international criminal law (ICL) courts only play a limited role in contributing to peace, reconciliation and fair reparations for victims in post-conflict societies;[12] as stated by Judge Van den Wyngaert and Judge Morrison, "international criminal law is concerned with individual responsibility and culpability and not with righting socio-historical wrongs".[13] Second, that fairness of proceedings and respect for human rights in all its aspects are necessary components to legitimacy of an international criminal tribunal, and that international criminal law (hereinafter 'ICL') courts should be expected to set the highest standards of fairness.[14]

All international and hybrid criminal tribunals that preceded the KSC contain in their Statutes provisions reflecting human rights and fair trial standards and have been set out to ensure a high standard of fairness in international criminal proceedings. At the same time, the practice of these international criminal tribunals has shown a more complex reality, in which relatively few

---

12   Rohan Colleen, "The Hybrid System of International Criminal Law: A Work in Progress or Just a Noble Experiment?" in Marina Aksenova, Elies van Sliedregt and Stephan Parmentier (eds), *Breaking the Cycle of Mass Atrocities: Criminological and Socio-Legal Approaches in International Criminal Law*, Hart Publishing, Oxford, 2019, at 96.

13   ICC, Prosecutor v. Jean-Pierre Bemba Gombo, Appeals Chamber Judgment on the appeal of Mr Jean-Pierre Bemba Gombo against Trial Chamber III's "Judgment pursuant to Article 74 of the Statute", 08 June 2018, ICC-01/05-01/08-3636-Anx2, Separate Opinion of Judge Van den Wyngaert and Judge Morrison, para. 76.

14   The author fully subscribes to what is stated in McDermott Yvonne, "The Right to a Fair Trial in International Criminal Law", PhD Thesis, National University of Ireland Galway, 2013, at 25: *"[...] the way in which the international community treats those accused of the gravest crimes known to mankind could be said to reflect the humanism of an international legal order. By granting accused individuals the procedural guarantees expected in the criminal justice system of any civilised nation, the international community shows that the international criminal law exercise is not one of mere retributivism. If they were to enunciate the highest standards of procedural fairness, international criminal tribunals would exercise a dual instrumentalist function in advancing the rule of law: first, they would show that no-one is above the law by placing despots and those who were in positions of great power on trial; second, they would show that everybody is entitled to the strongest of judicial guarantees and the right to a fair trial, regardless of the charges against them or their resources"*; see ICTY, *Prosecutor v. Dusko Tadić*, Appeals Chamber Decision on the Defence Motion for Interlocutory Appeal on Jurisdiction, 02 October 1995, IT-94-1-AR72, paras. 45-47; UN Doc S/25704, Report of the Secretary-General Pursuant to Paragraph 2 of the Security Council Resolution 808, 3 May 1993, para. 106.

and lengthy trials have taken place, and concerns as to the fairness of proceedings and the respect of the individuals involved there have been repeatedly raised.

While fairness is a result that can only be achieved in practice in light of the specific circumstances of each case, the legal framework of the institution clearly plays a central role to that end, by providing the rules to guide its work.

With this in mind, some observations are made in relation to the impact of some selected features of the KSC procedural framework with respect to the right to a fair trial, by comparing the KSC legal and procedural framework with that of other international criminal tribunals - mainly the International Criminal Court (hereinafter 'ICC') and the ICTY-ICTR (hereinafter 'ad hoc tribunals' or 'ad hocs').

Since the ICTY began its work in 1995, a number of different international and hybrid criminal courts have been created to bring criminal cases against individuals accused of having committed serious international crimes, slowly contributing to the development of a more or less coherent system of international criminal law. With its establishment and the commencement of its operation,[15] the Kosovo Specialist Chambers and Specialist Prosecutor's Office becomes an additional, contributing part of this system of law. It is therefore valuable to consider the KSC's legal and procedural framework within this broader context, in which different courts share many commonalities and to an extent influence each other.

---

15   At the time of writing, the KSC has ordered and the SPO has executed the arrest of two individuals, following the confirmation of their indictment: Salih Mustafa, arrested on 24 September 2020, and Nasim Haradinaj, arrested on 25 September 2020.

To this end, this contribution will first outline the main features of the procedural system adopted by the KSC, including the process of adoption of the rules and their review by the Constitutional Court.

It will then proceed by addressing the matters indicated above, as regulated by the Rules of Procedure and Evidence and the KSC Law where applicable. First, the relevant rules will be briefly outlined; then, a comparison with the correspondent rules of the *ad hoc* tribunals and/or the ICC will be drawn, where appropriate. Furthermore, some observations are made on the significance and potential impact of the discussed rules in light of the right to a fair trial in general and the specific rights and guarantees applicable in the relative context.

In particular, the rules on detention before and during trial and following acquittal are discussed because of the important pronouncements made by the Constitutional court in their regard in light of the right to liberty; the rules related to investigative measures, the indictment, disclosure obligations, dismissal of charges, and rules on evidence are discussed because of their important impact on the presumption of innocence, the right to be informed of their charges and the principle of equality of arms more broadly. Lastly, the figure of the Ombudsperson is briefly examined in relation to its potential to provide additional human rights protection for persons interacting with the KSC.

Part I

The Kosovo Specialist Chambers, between great expectations and negative auspices

by

Maria Stefania Cataleta

Author is grateful to the Humanitarian Law Center Kosovo for the interview and the University of Cambridge, in particular Prof. Toby Fenwick, for permission to use the course materials

To Paolo

1. Two ways to face mass atrocities

Since the end of WW II, the imperative was "never again" and a repeated question was what could be the response when mass atrocities occur? According to Art. 3 of the Universal Declaration of Human Rights (hereinafter 'UDHR') of 10 December 1948, *"Everyone has the right to life, liberty and security of person"*, all these rights cannot be violated with no actions to contrast such infringement. The day before the UDHR, the Genocide Convention was adopted, according to its Art. 1 *"The Contracting Parties confirm that genocide, whether committed in time of peace or in time of war, is a crime under international law which they undertake to prevent and to punish"*. Thus, it was established an active role by States against certain mass atrocities. It was the "never again" generation that enacted these new international legal rules that were coincident with new moral imperatives.

During the Post-Cold War, in 1990, President George H. W. Bush delivered a "New World Order" doctrine, speaking to the US Congress on 11 September, precisely 11 years before the World Trade Center attack. According to his doctrine, it was crucial to creating *"a world where the rule of law supplants the rule of the jungle [...] in which nations recognize the shared responsibility for freedom and justice [...] where the strong respect the rights of the weak"*. Nevertheless, in the 1990s, the genocides in Rwanda and Bosnia & Herzegovina were neither prevented nor stopped. The international community intervened only *ex post*, creating the ICTY and the ICTR in order to punish the major leaders responsible for the genocides. This was the first application of the duty to punish for mass atrocities at an international level where domestic justice was unable to do it.

In 1999, following the mass atrocities in Kosovo against the Albanian majority, the NATO air-strikes, which was an aggressive war against Serbia, was not sanctioned by the UN Security Council. According to the 'Goldstone report', the NATO action was "illegal but justified" and responded to the necessity to correct the failure of the UN Security Council to fulfil its mandate due to the vetoes in its decisions.

The military intervention in Kosovo was a humanitarian intervention. Many States, such as the Russian Federation, China and India contested the intervention in Kosovo and the Security Council did not authorise it because of such vetos. The R2P is a doctrine supporting the humanitarian intervention, given the *erga omnes* nature of the rules directed to protect fundamental human rights that the military intervention aims to safeguard. In this sense, the international community is entitled to intervene to stick up for them. The contrasting doctrine argues that if it is true that fundamental human rights are *jus cogens* also the prohibition of the use of force is *jus cogens* and there is not a priority order between different rules of *jus cogens*. All the more that the UN Charter prohibits the use of force and does not consent any humanitarian intervention. Another doctrine justifies the humanitarian intervention as a state of necessity, because in front of a humanitarian catastrophe it should be applied the broach *necessitas non habet legem*. Similarly, the theory concerning the concept of "human security" justifies the military intervention because the human security in action prevails over the State sovereignty. The R2P maintains that the international community is responsible to prevent, react and rebuilt when serious human rights violations, such as genocide, ethnic cleansing, crimes against humanity and war crimes occur in a State, mainly in a failed State, if this one is unable or unwilling to protect its population. Even if the R2P is controversial in literature and not supported by the UN Charter nor by traditional international law, it expresses an emerging rule of international law and a practice which is being consolidated in international relations.[16] (Focarelli, p. 617 et seq.)

The USA justified the military action underlining that resolutions 1160 and 1190 recalled Chapter VII of the UN Charter and this gave juridical legality and validity to the intervention. The atrocities committed by Serbs in Kosovo justified the humanitarian intervention because, face to a serious violation of the international law, any State member of the international community was enabled to intervene. The debate remains on the permission on the use of force without the Security Council authorization and far from the hypothesis of legitimate defence provided by the UN Charter. *Ex post* the NATO intervention was considered disproportionate, but the author dissent from this opinion. Even if the results were modest, something should be done to stop the massacres in front of the paralysis of the organ entitled to maintain the peace.[17]

On that occasion, the International Independent Commission on Kosovo declared that the experience from the NATO intervention in Kosovo suggested the need to close the gap between legality and legitimacy. The time was too ripe for the presentation of a principled framework for humanitarian intervention which could be used to guide future responses to imminent humanitarian catastrophes and which could be used to assess claims for humanitarian intervention.

---

16   Focarelli Carlo, *Diritto internazionale*, Wolters Kluwer, Milan, 2020, at 614 et seq.
17   *See generally* Sapienza Rosario, *Diritto internazionale. Casi e Materiali*, Giappichelli, Torino, 2002, at 201-202.

After the intervention in Kosovo, military intervention is allowed in extreme cases only and must follow six criteria: just cause, neutral evidence of the situation, right intention, last resort, proportional means, and reasonable prospects. These are the contemporary "just war" criteria.[18] There is a broad acceptance that intervention to stop genocide and mass crimes may be required even if action approved by the Security Council is blocked. The responsibility to protect (R2P) is a mean that proceeds in parallel with international justice to fight serious human rights violations. So, there are two fronts to combat mass atrocities: one military, a second one judiciary. Because the crimes under the KSC's jurisdiction were committed before, during and aftermath of the NATO air bombing, it was important to start from this tragic but salvific event for Kosovo.

Today, after the military intervention, Kosovo holds credible and relatively well-administered elections, but its institutions remain weak, and rampant corruption has given rise to deep public distrust in the government.[19] Journalists face serious pressure, and risk being attacked in connection with their reporting. The rule of law is inhibited by executive interference in the judiciary, as a consequence justice cannot be completely independent and impartial.[20] This is one important reason supporting the creation of the KSC. After the declaration of independence, on 17 February 2008, Kosovo was recognized as a sovereign State by many countries did not recognize it, such

18   Prof. Fenwick Toby, 'International Human Rights: war, conflict and the responsibility to protect' lecture, University of Cambridge, July 2020.
19   After the conflict, Kosovo was administrated through missions of State-building with the power to exercise full legislative, executive and judiciary powers. Unfortunately, often State-building missions created by the UN Security Council are not successful because they are an attempt to artificially impose political legitimacy without the use of common democratic instruments; as a result the State is not recognised by their citizens who do not obey it. After all they do not perceive it as a legitimate government, so the government is not effective. When the government is not effective there is the a lack of one of the elements of a State.
20   Freedom House Report, 2019.

as Serbia, China and Russia, because they believe that Kosovo is the result of the Western interventionism.[21] Today, it is the youngest country in Europe, but also one of the poorest. According to some historians, the ethnic polarization was the heart of the nationalism that the Western intervention has exacerbated instead to tone down.

---

21   The declaration of independence by the Kosovo Parliament rised the problem of premature recognition by other States. Premature recognition is discouraged in international law because it is perceived as an interference in the internal affairs and domestic jurisdiction. The independence of Kosovo was suddenly recognised by many countries, such as the United States and several countries of the EU, notwithstanding the Serbian protests since Kosovo was one of its provinces before the NATO intervention in 1999. The Russian Federation did not recognise the independence of Kosovo. Today, Kosovo is a member of the International Monetary Fund and World Bank Group, but it is not a UN member. In 2013, Kosovo stipulated with Serbia in Bruxelles a Treaty on the normalization of their mutual relations so that it can facilitate their admission in EU; *see* Focarelli, *supra* note 16, at 60.

2. The historical landscape and the KLA role in the Kosovo war

The KSC's specific and sensitive mandate to process only KLA's war criminals is considered in Kosovo as a selective and unfair example of justice that does not contribute to the normalization of the inter-ethnic relations nor to the dialogue between Serbia and Kosovo because only Albanians feel targeted. It is seen as an undemocratic and politicized body that increases the previous resentment against the ICTY, guilty of not having pursued enough prosecutions against Serbs allegedly responsible for war crimes committed against Albanians.

Now, the prosecution of only KLA's members exacerbates the Albanians' resentment and in this perspective, it is important, to understand the trials before the KSC, to know better the KLA and its role in the Kosovo war for independence.

The approach of the international community towards Kosovo depended on the fact that it has been considered for a long time an internal matter, as it was presented by Milošević and the Serb public opinion that saw the Albanians as usurpers of their sacred land, although they represented 90% of the population in Kosovo. The Albanians were not considered worthy of particular protection and consideration by the Milošević's regime. In the aim to strengthen the Serbian presence in the province, many discriminatory acts were enacted after 1989 against the Albanians, which were forbidden to trade any property without the permission of public authorities. A law limited the teaching of the Albanian language, history and literature at school. Police forces and the 'Božur', a Serbian armed movement, had a major power that they exercised in an unlimited way with judicial arrests, acts of tortures, mass summary trials and violent murders. The independence of Kosovo has deep roots. A huge popular protest was organized in 1988 asking the independence of Kosovo that, under Tito's regime, enjoyed a certain autonomy. On 27 February 1989, the state of emergency was established by Serbs during a season of social turbulences and disorders.[22]

The police oppression, facilitated by the public authorities, caused the displacement of thousands of Albanians who, on 2 July 1990, as a form of protest proclaimed the independence of Kosovo in the Parliament, eliminating any link with Serbia and demanding the right of self-determination. Belgrade reacted with a massive purge that involved about 115 000 Albanians, doctors, teachers and other professionals, who were dismissed. In response, the Kosovar leaders organised a secret referendum, to which participated 87,01% of the population, demanding independence from Yugoslavia, that the Parliament proclaimed without the recognition of the international community.

In 1992, Lord Carrington, Correspondent of the European Community tried a mediation, but Serbs refused being an internal affair of the Serbian Republic. In the meantime, the repression against the Albanian majority continued in the form of apartheid.[23] On 24 May 1992, secret elections were organized in Kosovo, plebiscitary were won by the Democratic League of Kosovo, founded by Ibrahim Rugova, a pacifist charismatic leader known as the "new Gandhi". He argued that it was essential to create an independent Kosovo politically and peacefully, avoiding an armed revolt against Serbs because it would be a bloodbath considering the disparity between the two forces.

---

22   *See generally* Pirjevec Jože, *Le guerre jugoslave,* Einaudi, Torino, 2014, at 554 et seq.
23   *See* Sapienza, *supra* note 17 at 194 et seq.

It was important to de-legitimize the undemocratic governmental institutions and internationalise the Kosovo question so that the international community could know the human rights violations against Albanians. Those created a shadow State that functioned almost clandestinely. On the opposite, according to the Serb's sentiment, the unique solution for the Kosovo problem was the expulsion of Albanians from Kosovo.

The armed mobilization of Kosovo started officially on 28 November 1997, at the funeral of Halit Gecaj. This event was transformed in a mass protest against the police violence and there, for the first time, some warriors with the Albanian uniform appeared publicly. From then on the fight for the independence of Kosovo was conducted by a national liberation movement, the Uçk (Ushtria Çlirimtare es Kosoves) or KLA, constituted by policemen, soldiers and students. Inspired by the Organization for the Liberation of Palestine, the KLA decided to reply to the violence with violence and organized a series of armed attempts against Serbs and compatriots perceived as traitors.[24] The protagonists of the war in Kosovo were young people; furthermore, it was the first war diffused on the internet at that time.

An armed revolt in Kosovo became reality at the end of the 1990's with the establishment of several KLA's training camps. Milošević replied with the iron fist. After the entered into the scene of the KLA and the Serbian violent reaction, the Kosovo question became international, as Rugova hoped.

From the mid '96 till February 1998, the KLA provoked about 100 armed

---

24   *See* Pirjevec, *supra* note 22, at 559 et seq. ; *see also*, Perrit Henry H. Jr., *Kosovo Liberation Army : the Inside Story of an Insurgency*, UI Press, Illinois, 2008.

attempts. During a massacre in the Drenica region by the Serbs, where 58 people lost their life, the historical leader of the KLA, Adem Jashari, was killed with almost all his family.[25] The fight against the KLA became indiscriminate, entire villages were set on fire with a wave of 17 000 refugees. Many young people became members of the KLA, which were composed of about 12 000 warriors, later become 40-50 000. The armed revolt would have conducted to the liberation of Kosovo and its union with the motherland, the Albania.[26]

Following to the Drenica outbreak of violences, the ICTY's Prosecutor, Louise Arbour, announced the possible impeachment of responsible people, including Milošević, who continued to maintain that the Kosovo problem was an internal matter. The international community, through Felipe Gonzáles, was trying to mediate between the Serb authorities and the Albanian political representatives.

At the American State Secretary Madeleine Albright's hostility towards the Serbs was opposed to the traditional filo-Serb attitude of Europe, especially Paris, Moscow and Rome because of their economic interests. The news about the cruel repression circulated from late 1997 to the beginning of 1998. Security Council Resolution 1160 (1998) deplored the Serb Army"s excessive use of violence as well as the KLA's terrorist attempts. Unfortunately, the resolution did not address in depth the origin of the revolt in Kosovo, but exhorted FRY and Kosovars to cooperate for a peaceful resolution of the crisis, preserving the sovereignty and territorial integrity of the FRY. The resolution invited the Prosecutor of the ICTY to investigate crimes committed

---

25   ICTY, *Prosecutor v. Vlastimir Dordević*, Case No. IT-05-87/1-T, Trial Judgment, Volume I of II, 23 February 2011, para. 271.
26   Pirjevec, *supra* note 22.

during the violence in Kosovo.[27]

Milošević, with the pretext to fight against the KLA separatist terrorists, who put at risk the "peaceful" domestic partnership of different ethnicities in Kosovo province, refused the external interference and deployed in the province 25 000 policemen and 30 000 soldiers with tanks, heavy artillery and helicopters to sedate the revolt. They assaulted Dečani, burned a large part of the town and plundered the population for five days, interrupting any link between the central Kosovo and Albania. According to the UNHCR data, 42 000 people were forced to run away towards Albania and Montenegro. The violence caused a large eco in international media, but the Serbs reacted affirming paradoxically that the same Albanians had burned their homes and villages, killed and pushed their people to flight with the only aim to discredit the Serb's reputation.[28]

Kosovo was living a terrible experience. *"On television were transmitted only images of destruction and death. Psychiatrists announced and enunciated catastrophic forecasts. The levels of post-traumatic stress disorder would have been dramatically high and Kosovars would have had been taken care of for generations. The largest part of humanitarian organizations that had obtained founds sent doctors, psychiatrists, psychologists, to care directly a population labelled as sick, traumatized [...] collective traumas so widespread cannot be interpreted and treated as phenomenons confined in an individual and pathological dimension [...]".[29]*

Other UN Security Council resolutions were adopted, n. 1199 (1998) and n.

---

27   *See* Sapienza, *supra* note 17.
28   *See* Pirjevec, *supra* note 22 at 559 et seq.
29   *See* Losi Natale, *Critica del trauma,* Quodlibet Studio, Macerata, 2020, at 67-73.

1203 (1998), defining the situation in Kosovo as a "humanitarian disaster" and a threat to international peace and security. Following the explosion of violence, in 1999, the Council of NATO started to consider a military intervention in Kosovo and with the military maneuvers called "Determined Falcon", where 83 planes were implied, gave a message to Milošević. Indeed, Russia would have imposed a veto within the Security Council against any military intervention under the aegis of the UN.

Belgrade authorized the Kosovo Diplomatic Observer Mission, formed by accredited diplomats charged to visit the province and observe the local situation, that confirmed the continuous human rights violations against Albanians. In the meantime, the Serb police forces and army were involved to impede that the KLA transformed itself from an armed movement into a paramilitary army. For some, the KLA was a terrorist movement but not for the USA, whose representatives of the Clinton administration met the leaders of the movement, which was accepted as a reality enjoying the largest Albanian popular support. According to them, an organization that had some terrorists was not necessarily terrorist *per se*.[30]

The USA Senate voted a motion inviting Clinton to bring Milošević to justice before the ICTY for war crimes. NATO's intervention in Kosovo was strongly supported by Madeleine Albright as an act of "democratic interventionism". In the American opinion, the humanitarian crisis in Kosovo was sufficient for a military intervention, even without the authorization of the UN Security Council. Moreover, the UN Charter justified the use of force only in case of self-defence or after the Security Council authorization, so to maintain or

---

30   *See* Caplan Richard, *International Diplomacy and the Crisis in Kosovo*, in 'International Affairs', vol. 74, n. 4, August 1998, at 758.

restore peace. However, according to the opinion in favour of the intervention, a "humanitarian intervention" did not need the Security Council authorization, because it was decided to carry out the Security Council previous resolutions.

In the meantime of the international debate about the NATO intervention, after the defeat of Junik, in August '98, a stronghold for the KLA, 160 000 Albanians were forced to escape in the bush, with neither water nor food. In that period, according to a report of Human Rights Watch, 1 500 Kosovars were killed, 45 000 houses were destroyed, about 500 villages were set on fire. This situation strengthened the idea of the military intervention facing the diplomatic failure to join an agreement on the Kosovo autonomy.

The UN Security Council resolution 1199 (1998) demanding the stop of the violence was considered a watershed of the attitude of the international community towards the humanitarian crisis in Kosovo. Milošević adduced that the origin of the war was the Albanian separatism and terrorism, but faced with his intransigence to deal, on 24 September, the Council of the Atlantic Alliance authorized the supreme chief to send an alert, the so-called Activation Warning – ACTWARN, that forecasted a limited intervention in Kosovo. It was the first step towards the use of air raids in a moment during which other massacres were in progress, such as in Drenica, where 19 Albanians were killed by the police forces who had killed the victims, within who women and children, with a blow to the neck while they were getting away.

Milošević did not respect Security Council resolution 1199, that imposed him to retire the special troops from Kosovo, neither punished the Serbs responsible for new massacres. Without the withdrawal of his troops, the NATO air raid would be enacted. Milošević did not accept Hill's Plan on his retirement from Kosovo. This compromise was also refused from the KLA, contrary to any deal with Belgrade and whose popularity grew to such an extent to attract many young people. They obtained weapons by the USA, German and Croatian intelligence on the promise to refuse any contact with the Islamic fundamentalists.

The persecutions against Albanians continued while they hoped for the NATO's intervention. Many attacks against Albanian villages were conducted by the police, gifted with heavy armaments, with ten murders and 5 500 fugitives from the zone of Podujevë. In the early '99 the situation got worse and in fact, on 15 January, there was a slaughter in Račak, in central Kosovo, organized by the special forces as retaliation for the assassination of three men by the KLA. In this event, 45 unarmed civilians were killed on a hill, the oldest was 99 and the youngest 14 years old, after having been tortured and mutilated.[31]

After the Račak slaughter, Milošević was no longer seen by the American diplomacy as an interlocutor do deal with but as an evil to be eradicated, also after the failure of the *Rambouillet* negotiations, that Belgradese media presented as a great victory for Milošević's. A referendum for the Kosovo independence was no longer foreseen, but only a self-government. Nevertheless, the Serbs did not accept the peace proposal coming from *Rambouillet* and the intervention of foreign troops in Kosovo. Warrants of arrest were launched by the Serb Ministry of Intern against eight "Albanians separatist and terrorist", included Hashim Thaçi, at that time a candidate for

---

31   *See* Pirjevec, *supra* note 22 at 583-587.

the presidency of the provisional government of Kosovo, Jakup Krasniqui and Sulejman Selimi, the new commander of the KLA.

Despite the peace negotiations, the Serb offensive involved the region of Kosovska Mitrovica, from where 20 000 people were kicked out of their houses and entire villages set on fire. 40 000 Serbs with 300 tanks used the strategy to indiscriminately kill, rape and plunder in order to terrorize the civilians and force them to flight. A climate of hatred dominated. In the towns, the Albanians had no food because the Serbs refused to sell them the necessary for the subsistence and no water because the water well had been poisoned with dead bodies and carrions. If the lords of war wanted to save someone, they marked the house with an "S".[32] The Serb propaganda presented the *Rambouillet* agreement as a threat to the Serb population, compared with the Jews persecution under the Nazis. To avoid their holocaust, they should oppose to their enemies, first of all the USA, with every means.

On 23 March, the President of EU, Javier Solana, announced the Operation "Allied Force". For the first time, NATO, created with defensive proposal against attacks towards their own members States, was engaged in an offensive operation against a sovereign State. This violated its same constitution and the UN Charter, because the fate of the Albanian population, victim of ethnic cleansing, the security and stability of the NATO zone and all Europe were considered to be in danger. It was also a message to all the dictators in the world that the most serious crimes against humanity would not remain unpunished.[33]

---

32   *Id.*, at 599-601.
33   « Der Spiegel », n 1, 2000, at 134.

The air raids started at 8:00pm of the 24th March with the employment of 80 planes made available by 13 NATO's members; they were directed against the Milošević's regime and not against the Serbian population and focused on the military installations in Kosovo and Central Serbia. The regime denounced the aggression and proclaimed the state of war, during which all civil rights were abolished. The radio and television were closed, except those under the authorities' control.

There were two wars,[34] one on the sky and the second one on the land, where the ethnic cleansing intensified against the "rebel" Albanians and the KLA members. People escaped chaotically towards Albania, Macedonia and Montenegro in hostile weather conditions with very low temperatures mainly during the night. This was an occasion for the authorities to evacuate completely the Albanians from Kosovo. The KLA tried to resist, offering protection to the population but with few means and with no strong command chain. They were exterminated or forced to escape, after having asked in vain to the West the weapons necessary to fight.

In the meantime, in Serbia the propaganda machine lighted patriotism and atavistic nationalism against an illegal and unjustified aggression against a sovereign State founder member of UN. According to the propaganda, the Albanian fugitives escaped from the NATO air bombing and not from the ethnic cleansing, that was an invention of Western media that had paid the fugitives to declare that they were victims of atrocities. To the NATO attack Milošević replied with a demographic explosion of a biblical exodus, while the massacres and expulsion of civilians continued. The call for mobilization to fight, done by the KLA to men from 18 to 50 years old, did not have any

---

34   « Der Spiegel », n 2, 2000, at 136.

effect on a terrified population.

At the beginning of April the fugitives were 262 000 in Albania only, with no adequate humanitarian assistance, no food and no accommodation. In Macedonia, where the fugitives were 115-120 000, the government ordered to close the borders. Following this decision, 65 000 evacuee people were stopped at the border of Bllacë in train wagons under the rain. When they were finally welcomed, after Western powers pressure, they were 25 000. In the summer of '98, from the beginning of the Kosovo crisis, 1 100 000 had been forced to flee.[35] The NATO accused Milošević and other officials of war crimes, but the violence of the Yugoslavian army did not stop. The exodus caused many criticisms also against NATO and USA, accused of causing this because of their aggression, in contrast with international law and the UN Charter law. It was defined as the "Madeleine's war".

The Yugoslavian government, facing the strong reaction that the enormous exodus had in the West, blocked the borders and in so doing forced the refugees to stay encamped near the borders or to come back to Kosovo where they can be used by Serbs as human shields.

On 7 April, the German Defence Minister, Rudolf Scharping, revealed that the so- called "Horseshoe" plan was orchestrated by the authorities of Belgrade since 1998 aiming to empty Kosovo from the hated ethnicity. During the air bombing, the Serbs had taken profit to enact a systematic and massive ethnic cleansing. More that 300 villages had been plunder and burned and a large part of the Albanian intelligentsia in Kosovo had been

---

35   *See generally*, Petrungaro Stefano, *Balcani. Una storia di violenza?*, Carocci, Rome, 2012.

eliminated. The atrocities against the Albanians and the presence of mass graves were denounced by the General Secretary before the Commission for Human Rights, which affirmed that a new international rule was emerging against the violent repression of minorities whose defence should prevail over national sovereignty.[36]

Facing the Serb resistance and after three weeks of bombings, on 12 April, the KLA spokesman, Jakup Krasniqui, met in Brussels the USA Secretary of State, Madeleine Albright. According to the Daily Telegraph, some secret agreements were in progress between USA and the KLA in order to arm it. In the meantime, the air raids intensified from the original 8 hours during the night to an uninterrupted daily campaign not only against military targets but also against civil infrastructures necessary to the military actions. The intention was to attack the morale of the population to provoke a reaction against Milošević. But in this way the NATO air attacks caused also civil casualties, like the attack against a train full of civilians and against the Chinese Embassy. At the end of the military intervention about 500 deaths and 8 000 injured were the collateral civil damages.[37] Following the NATO air bombings, the violence did not refrain but multiplied.

On 6 May, on Petersberg mountain, near Bonn, an agreement was signed concerning the immediate cessation of the military operations, the retire of the Serb regular and irregular forces and the demilitarization of the KLA. This would have consented the return of the refugees and the start of a process of self-government, in the respect of the sovereignty and territorial integrity of Yugoslavian Federation. But the military escalation did not stop.

---

36   Pirjevec, *supra* note 22 at 619.
37   *Id.*

On 27 May, the Prosecutor of the ICTY issued a warrant against Milošević and four other exponents of his regime as responsible for crimes against humanity and war crimes. In this way the Prosecutor, Mrs. Louise Arbour, prevented that the *vožd* could enjoy immunity in a future peace negotiation. On 2 June, in sooth, Milošević signed a peace agreement including the *Rambouillet* requests, but with no mention of the independence of Kosovo. On 3 June, the Serb Parliament accepted the peace plan. The agreement was finally signed on 9 June in Kumanovo. The air bombings were interrupted after 79 days. With the resolution 1244 the UN Security Council legitimated *ex post* the NATO intervention and transformed Kosovo in an international protectorate that should allow Kosovar refugees to come back.[38] This, however, had not impeded the ethnic cleansing.*"The Serbs finish 'their' war how they started it, with crime and horror".*[39]

Solana affirmed that the use of force in Kosovo without the UN Security Council mandate remained an exception and was not the expression of a new international law. With the arrival in Kosovo of 14 000 soldiers of the KFOR also a counter-exodus of Albanian exiles started from Albania, Macedonia and Montenegro, they were about 300 000 people. But an exodus of at least 165 000 Serbs from Kosovo started at the same time. Notwithstanding, at Javier Solana's promises that, if remained in Kosovo, Serbs would have been protected, they were target of revenge and violence. The KLA, with 20 000 members, did not deliver the weapons and did not renounce to the revenge. A problem was the possible dissolution of the KLA, considered a destabilizing factor in the region. Some commanders, such as Hashim Thaçi, strongly

---

38   NATO justified the intervention by claiming that it derived its mandate *ex post facto* from UN Security Resolution 1244(1999) which was adopted on 10 June 1999. *See* NATO website, "NATO's role in Kosovo", https://www.nato.int/cps/en/natolive/topics 48818.htm (accessed, January 15, 2021).
39   Le Monde, 12 December 1995.

refused any demilitarization, but in the end they accepted some conditions.

The exhortation of Solana to the Albanians to not commit acts of revenge had fallen on deaf ears in a society victim of a century of humiliating sufferings and where revenge is a moral imperative. The action of the KSC is focused on this segment of illegal actions. Were these acts of violence enough to create a new international tribunal?

3. The path towards a new Court

Accompanying the dissolution of the former Yugoslavia, Kosovo's war of independence caused enormous casualties, war crimes, ethnic cleansing and international interventions. More that 13 000 people died, most of them ethnic Albanians, precisely 80 per cent, while 16 per cent were members of the ethnic Serb minority, and 4 per cent were Roma, Bosniaks and members of other minority communities in Kosovo.[40]

The conflict ended in June 1999 with the NATO air bombardments against the Yugoslavian Army and allied police forces accused of committing atrocities against ethnic Albanian civilians, while around 45 per cent of ethnic Serb casualties of the war were military and police personnel. The Albanian community was the target of a state-orchestrated ethnic cleansing plan, aiming also to contrast the demand for self-determination and independence of Kosovo. The alleged war crimes and crimes against humanity committed were prohibited by the international criminal law, international humanitarian law and law of armed conflict, by virtue of this they had been judicially pursued.

Today, a sentiment of frustration and resentment for the past atrocities continues to crush the peace and the intra-ethnic and inter-ethnic reconciliation process within Kosovo and between Kosovo and Serbia, due to the absence of a peace agreement between the two countries. The complex legacies of the conflict had activated a transitional justice process sponsored from outside and resulted in ad *hoc judicial* mechanisms, launching first and

---

40   Humanitarian Law Center Kosovo, 'The Kosovo Memory Book', Pristina, 2011, available at http://www.kosovomemorybook.org.org (accessed May 28, 2020).

most importantly the ICTY, but also domestic hybrid mechanisms such as the UNMIK.

The UNMIK has administered domestic hybrid courts in Kosovo prosecuting few low-profile war criminals, about 40 war crimes cases. However, it was considered ineffective, residual and with many deficiencies such as the insufficient protection measures for witnesses and judges. It has reduced its presence in Kosovo after Kosovo's declaration of independence, in 2008, and has handed the EULEX information regarding a large number of suspected war crimes; its activity of investigation was hindered by its same limited legal and territorial jurisdiction and from the absence of cooperation from Serbia. In 2014, it has limited its presence in Kosovo, reducing *de facto* the investigations.

On the other hand, the ICTY has judged 161 war criminals and its jurisdiction has covered the entire territory of the former Yugoslavia. Concerning Kosovo, it has examined many high-ranking Serb military and political officials and managed only two high profile cases against two KLA commanders, namely Ramush Haradinaj and Fatmir Limaj, later both of them acquitted. In the opinion of Albanians in Kosovo, ICTY has not prosecuted enough Serbs; some consider it an anti-Serb tribunal because the largest part of the proceedings concerned Serbs.

This external or quasi-external transitional justice mechanisms were necessary because of the reluctance of domestic courts to prosecute war criminals in Kosovo, due to the lack of effective protection measures for judges and prosecutors and for fears of political retaliation for prosecuting former KLA members, now powerful political leaders. At the same time, many civilian victims remain dissatisfied because they complain limited access to reparations, although many restorative justice initiatives carried out, such as the establishment of the Government Commission on Missing Persons in 2008 or the provision of reparations in the form of pensions to KLA war veterans.[41] In 2012, was established an Inter-Ministerial Working Group on Dealing with the Past and Reconciliation (hereinafter 'IMWG'), that however was slightly supported by the Government.

Thus, coherently with the transitional justice process, several initiatives were put in place but they had modest results. International and hybrid courts were perceived as a mere instrument of criminal justice, insufficient to provide other forms of transitional justice finalities, such as victim support and reconciliation; so they were judged more oriented on retributive than restorative justice. *"The unintended consequence of international criminal justice in Kosovo and Serbia has been the glorification of the respective perpetrators and marginalization of the respective victims".*[42]

The vision of this paper is that this is not the failure of international criminal justice. In fact, the discontent in Kosovo is entrenched because every effort to deal with the past, in every forms it is conducted, is condemned to the failure because communities constantly reject any attempt of reconciliation promoted both from external and internal actors. Every mechanism or other instruments of transitional justice is criticized and de-legitimized by the population and by the same political class. Moreover, immobility cannot be

---

41   *See generally* Humanitarian Law Center Kosovo, 'War Reparations for Civilian Victims: What Access for Communities?', Pristina, 30 November 2016, available online at http://hlc-kosovo.org/?wpdmdl=4975 (accessed May 28, 2020).

42   *See* Visoka Gëzim, "Assessing the potential impact of the Kosovo Specialist Court", Impunity Watch, Pax, The Netherland, 2017, at 16, available online: https://www.paxforpeace.nl (accessed May 29, 2020); *see also* of the same author "Arrested Truth: Transitional Justice and the Politics of Remembrance in Kosovo", *Journal of Human Rights Practice*, Vol. 8, No. 1, 2016, at 62-80.

justified in this difficult setting. For this reason, it is not correct to say that nothing has been done.

This is the thorny and ruinous background that has anticipated the creation of the KSC, criticized even before its establishment and beginning of its work and giving way to the criticism that both national and international actors share the same responsibility for "mismanaging" the transitional justice process in Kosovo.[43]

---

43   Visoka, Assessing the potential impact of the Kosovo Specialist Court, *id.*

4. The European and international pressures

The necessity to establish a hybrid tribunal for the crimes committed in Kosovo emerged in 2011, when the so-called 'Marty Report' was published subsequently to the investigation conducted under the aegis of the CoE. The Report was issued by the Council of Europe's Parliamentary Assembly and released on 7 January 2011. It was based on the work of the Council of Europe's Parliamentary Committee on Legal Affairs and Human Rights, which appointed, in 2008, the Swiss senator Dick Marty as a rapporteur to investigate certain crimes.[44] Subsequently, the CoE recommended Kosovo to cooperate with the EULEX, in order to seriously and independently investigate and prosecute people responsible for the alleged atrocities.[45]

As emerged, the crimes concerned especially organ harvesting, allegations already formulated, in her memoirs, by the then ICTY Prosecutor Carla del Ponte against mid- and senior level KLA officers,[46] including Ramush and Daut Haradinaj, suspected of international crimes against Serbs and Albanians who had remained in Kosovo at the end of the conflict between the KLA and the Serbian government. The suspected would have been involved in the abduction of hundreds of persons, mainly ethnic Serbs, to the mountains of northern Albania, where some of them were said to have been killed at a Yellow House in Rripë for the extraction of their organs which

---

44   Report 'Inhuman treatment of people and illicit trafficking in human organs in Kosovo' released on 12 December 2010 by the Special Rapporteur for the CoE's Committee on Legal Affairs and Human Rights. Council of Europe Parliamentary Assembly, Committee on Legal Affairs and Human Rights, AS/Jur (2010) 46 of 12 December 2010.
45   Resolution 1782 (2011) of 25.1.2011 of the Parliamentary Assembly of the Council of Europe, para 1. Council of Europe, Parliamentary Assembly, Report Doc. 12462 7 January 2011, available online at www.assembly.coe.int (accessed April 29, 2020).
46   C. Del Ponte Carla/Sudetic Chuck, "Madame Prosecutor: Confrontations with Humanity's Worst Criminals and the Culture of Impunity", Kindle Edition, 2008.

were to be sold on the black market. The Chairman of the Association for Missing Persons from Kosovo, Ranko Djinović, accused the KLA leaders, including Hashim Thaçi. The allegations over these crimes had remained unpunished as the ICTY and UNMIK had been unable to gather sufficient evidence, given the fact that no witnesses had come forward, no bodies had been discovered and there were no further leads connecting high-ranking members of the KLA to these alleged crimes. The ICTY Office of the Prosecutor did not transfer the case to UNMIK.

These allegations reversed the national narrative on the Kosovo Albanian's liberation fight against the Serbs, seen no more as oppressors but as victims of the crimes committed by the KLA. In fact, prisoners belonging to ethnic minorities, Serbs and Kosovo Albanian collaborators with Serbs or simply political opponent would have been detained in secret centres under KLA control and would have disappeared, after been subjected to inhuman and degrading treatments. Then, after killing, organs would have been removed from some prisoners and taken abroad for transplantation. The 'Marty Report' indicated certain KLA members (mainly from the Drenica region) as authors of these crimes against wartime detainees (before June 1999) and post-war detainees (after June 1999). Various were the reasons for such crimes, as revenge, punishment and profit. The accused would have organised a network of detention facilities in northern Albania for unlawful activities.

The idea that such terrible crimes were not properly investigated caused great debate within the international community and that is why the Council of Europe appointed senator Dick Marty as Special Rapporteur to lead an investigation in order to verify the veracity of such allegations, deliver justice to the victims and bring the responsible to justice.

Initially, the 'Marty Report' did not promote the creation of a new judicial organ, asking EU member States and EULEX to allocate resources and confirm political support for investigating those war crimes while offering protection to the witnesses threatened in Kosovo. At that time the option to give the mandate to ICTY and EULEX to prosecute such allegation was rejected because: firstly, the ICTY was finishing its functions and its competence *ratione loci* and *temporis* did not cover allegations related to the post-conflict period and in northern Albania, but just during the war and in the territory of the former Yugoslavia; while EULEX lacked resources and competence to carry out a proper criminal justice process.

Moreover, in 2011, the EU created the SITF with the mandate to conduct independent and objective investigations over the 'Marty Report' allegations, while, in the meantime, the EU was concluding the first agreement for the normalization of relations between Kosovo and Serbia. After two and a half years, SITF Prosecutor Clint Williamson issued the preliminary findings, that were in line with most of the 'Marty Report' allegations against KLA's senior officials.

The 'Marty Report' claimed to have found evidence of an *ad hoc* detention network consisting of six or seven separate facilities that was run by the KLA on Albanian territory ; they were used during the final months of the Kosovo war in the period between April and mid-June 1999 and those that became operative after the armed conflict had ended in the period between mid-June 1999 and August 2000. The victims allegedly taken to the wartime detention facilities were mostly ethnic Albanians suspected of collaboration with the Serbs, who were arrested for the purpose of interrogation. Many of them were said to have been beaten or even tortured, even if most of them survived. The victims claimed to have been held detained at the post-conflict detention facilities were mainly ethnic Serbs who disappeared. The Report alleged also that a very limited number of such victims were killed for the extraction of their kidneys, not at the Yellow House in Rripë, which on the contrary served as a way station, but at a farmhouse in Fushë-Krujë close to the airport. Thus, these allegations were confirmed except the organ harvesting and trafficking, a practice occurred on a very limited scale, according to the evidence.[47]

Following the 'Marty Report', the international community asked the Government of Kosovo to establish a special court aiming to prosecute individuals responsible for these war crimes, ensure justice for the victims and conduct the country towards a transitional process necessary to guarantee stability. The pressure involved also the US that envisaged even the UN's intervention if Pristina had failed to approve a "new EU-backed court soon". Several EU member States and the US openly prospected that if Kosovo's institutions had failed to establish a special arrangement integrated within Kosovo's legal system, the consequence was that the UN Security Council would authorise the creation of a UN special court outside Kosovo's jurisdiction.[48]

---

47   SITF, 'Statement of the Chief Prosecutor of the Special Investigative Task Force', Brussels, 29 July 2014, at. 3, available at http://www.balkaninsight.com/en/file/show/Statement_of_the_ChiefProsecutor_of_the_SITF_EN.pdf (accessed June 04, 2020).
48   "US ambassador Tracey Ann Jacobson said on Thursday that the United States could not continue to block attempts by permanent UN Security Council member Russia to form a tribunal for Kosovo if Pristina fails to approve the formation of the new special court to try senior Kosovo Liberation Army figures for serious crimes during and after the 1998-1999 war", Balkan Transitional Justice, Una Hajdar, 'US Warns Kosovo: Approve New War Court Quickly', 17 April 2015, available online at http://www.balkaninsight.com (accessed June 04, 2020).

For some experts, an internationalized organ, formally attached to the Kosovo legal system but physically located outside Kosovo, was considered more appropriate to prevent the risks of corruption and politicization of domestic courts, judged inadequate and unfair. For some others, the main reason for choosing an *ad hoc* internationalized tribunal was the negative impact of Kosovo population towards the 'Marty Report', alongside the weak judicial capacity for prosecuting war crimes and the fragile witness protection measures offered at local level. As a matter of fact, the CoE Parliamentary Assembly pointed out that the crimes allegedly committed had not been pursued in the country.

Following the international investigations, on 4 September 2012, the President of the Republic of Kosovo sent a letter to the EU High Representative, inviting her to continue the presence of EULEX notwithstanding the Kosovo independence (fully achieved in September 2012), formally legitimizing the SITF action. On the same date, the response was ratified by the Assembly of Kosovo as an international agreement with the EU.

Moreover, on 14 April 2014, the President of the Republic of Kosovo, Atifete Jahjaga, before the expiry of the EULEX mission in June 2014, invited again the EU High Representative to extend the EULEX mandate of two more years, until June 2016, expressly asking that a special court within the Kosovo judicial system, described in detail in the letter, would prosecute the accusations emerged from the SITF investigations. On the same 14 April 2014, the High Representative accepted the invitation and confirmed that the

SITF would have continued its activity until the end of the investigations.[49]

Also this exchange of letter, similarly to the previous once, was ratified by the Kosovo Assembly as an international agreement between Kosovo and EU.[50] The exchange of letters was also adopted as a law by the Assembly of Kosovo on 23 April 2014. These two circumstances mark the institutional commitment taken on different occasions by Kosovo to support the establishment of the KSC. The formal expression of consent by the Kosovo institutional representatives with the subsequent obligation to respect two different international agreements, supports the thesis about the legitimacy of the KSC.

On July, the SITF Lead Prosecutor communicated an indictment against some members of the KLA, responsible for crimes against humanity, war crimes and some violations of the Kosovo law for having targeted Serbs, Roma, collaborators of Serbs, opponents of the KLA and other minority populations in Kosovo with acts of persecution like unlawful killings, abductions, enforced disappearances, illegal detentions in camps in Kosovo and Albania, sexual violence, other forms of inhuman treatments, forced displacements of individuals from their home, and desecration and destruction of churches.[51] The widespread organ trafficking, the main allegation of the 'Marty Report', was not supported by enough evidence. So, while the ICTY had prosecuted mainly Serbian officials and had not covered the post-war period, the KSC

---

49   Letter of High Representative of the European Union, Catherine Ashton, dated 14 April 2014.
50   Law No. 04/L-274 on the Ratification of the International Agreement between the Republic of Kosovo and the European Union on the European Union Rule of Law Mission in Kosovo of 15 May 2014 and Annexed Exchange of Letters, Pristina, 23 April 2014, at 3; available online at: www.kuvendikosoves.org/common/docs/ligjet/04-L-274%20a.pdf (accessed April 20, 2020).
51   Report (S/2014/558) of the Secretary General to the Security Council of 1 August 2014, at 18.

will judge only Kosovo Albanian KLA senior officials. Thus, the President of the Republic of Kosovo invited the EU to assist his country in the institution of a new court within the Kosovo judicial system.[52]

Notwithstanding the opposition of the Kosovo Albanian political parties, in March 2015, the Government amended the Constitution permitting the creation of the KSC by the Assembly. The approval of two constitutional amendments, on 7 March 2015 and the following judgement of the Constitutional Court (promoted by the President of Kosovo for reviewing and avoiding any legal and political uncertainty) affirming that those amendments respected the human rights and fundamental freedoms contained in the same Constitution (and derived from the international agreement between Kosovo and EU),[53] show the political consent and the legality supporting the creation of the KSC, even if the internal political debate was intense.

Coherently with the legality of the procedure, finally the Kosovo Assembly voted in favour of the Court with a two-thirds majority of the elected representatives. It is important to underline that the Assembly is a political organ composed of the elected representatives of the population. This aspect cannot be underestimated in terms of local ownership as well.

The establishment of the new Court coincided with the time that a EULEX led panel issued the verdict for the high-profile trial of 15 former KLA affiliated, well known as the 'Drenica Group'. This trial was very discussed, suspected to be highly politicized and afflicted by public protests and witnesses intimidation. This was the climate in Kosovo in which criminal law

---

52   Letter of the President of Republic of Kosovo dated 14 April 2014.
53   Judgment of the Constitutional Court of the Republic of Kosovo in Case No. KO26/15 of 15 April 2015.

was administrated.

Finally, the KSC and the Specialist Prosecutor's Office were created by Law No. 05/L-053, adopted on 3 August 2015 by the Assembly of the Republic of Kosovo, enacted on 15 September 2015.[54] Thus, this Law on the creation of the KSC was adopted to enable the agreement between UE and Kosovo.[55]

On the same date of the adoption, the Assembly approved the Constitutional amendment No. 24, reforming the Kosovo Constitution with a new article, No. 162, authorizing the creation of an *ad hoc* judicial body within the domestic legal system.[56] The constitutional amendment states that the KSC shall *"have full legal and juridical personality"* and *"all the necessary powers and mandate for their operation, judicial co-operation, assistance, witness protection, security, detention and the service of sentence outside the territory of Kosovo for anyone convicted".*[57] The Law stipulated that, as an international obligation, the KSC will *"secure independent, impartial, fair and efficient criminal proceedings in relation to allegations of grave transborder and international crimes committed during and in the aftermath of the conflict in Kosovo"* reported by the 'Marty Report' and by the SITF.[58]

Some perceived that the hypothetical failure of legislative procedure would have meant a threat to Kosovo's EU integration process and the visa

---

54   Available online at: www.kuvendikosoves.org (accessed April 20, 2020).
55   Art. 1(2) of the Law No. 05/L-053 of 3 August 2015.
56   Amendment to the Constitution of the Republic of Kosovo No. 05-D-139 of 3.8.2015, available at: http://gzk.rks-gov.net (accessed May 11, 2020).
57   Assembly of Kosovo, 'Amendment of the Constitution of the Republic of Kosovo', Doc. No. 05-D-139, 3 August 2015, available at http://www.kuvendikosoves.org/common/docs/Amendment%20of%20the%20Constitution%20-no%2024.pdf (accessed June 04, 2020).
58   Assembly of Kosovo, 'Law No. 05/L-053 on the Specialist Chambers and Specialist Prosecutor's Office', Art. 1.

liberalization regime.[59] However, it is important to underline that there were two different legislative interventions, an ordinary law and a constitutional one. The creation of this new judicial organ was so important and largely considered appropriate for several reasons that it was necessary to add a new article to the Constitution. Both normative sources refer to the complaints and recommendations contained in the 'CoE Report'.

Thus, the legal base of the new Court is contained in different normative sources: a constitutional one, that is the Constitution of the Republic of Kosovo, more precisely, the new Art. 24; an ordinary one, the Law No. 05/L-053 of 2015 on Specialist Chambers and Specialist Prosecutor's Office; finally, an international one, the international treaty legally binding the Republic of Kosovo and the EU, ratifying twice an exchange of letters between the President of Kosovo and the EU High Representative on date 14 April 2014.[60] This argument confirms the assumption about the legitimacy of the KSC, due to the formal and substantial regularity of its creating procedure.

---

59   *See* Muharremi, *supra* note 7 at 977.
60   The letters of the President of the Republic of Kosovo were joined to the agreement.

5. The mixed nature of the KSC

In order to fulfil its mandate, the Court has been granted full diplomatic privileges, immunities and facilities in the Netherlands, where is it located according to an agreement signed between the Government of Kosovo and the Kingdom of the Netherlands on 15 February 2016. The location outside Kosovo was necessary primarily because of the international community's fears that criminal trials in Kosovo would not produce meaningful results as the convicted persons are part of Kosovo's establishment and are so influential and powerful that they could hinder justice at a domestic level.

The KSC is attached to the Kosovo judicial system (this is one of the national aspects: the KSC are a Kosovo judicial body), composed by the Basic Court, the Court of Appeals, the Supreme Court and the Constitutional Court. Only international judges serve the KSC. The Head of EULEX is the Appointing Authority for the judges, who are 19 with the President.

The Court comprises two main organs: the Chambers and the Registry. The Chambers consist of the President of the Chambers and individual judges attached to each level of the court system in Kosovo. The Court is staffed entirely by non Kosovars (this is one of the international aspects of the Court) because of the sensitive nature of the trials, that demand impartiality from the judges. Indeed, the inclusion of local staff would have harmed the investigative activity and maybe conditioned the verdicts. Naturally, also this exclusion of national personnel has provoked heated reactions in Kosovo and increased hostility towards the KSC.

The Specialist Prosecutor is an independent organ and does not receive instructions from any government or any other source. Furthermore, he does not share any information with Kosovo authorities. He is appointed by the Head of EULEX and he is the Lead Prosecutor of the SITF, he has a police service and a qualified staff. The Registry includes a Defence Office, a Victims Participation Office, a Witness Protection and Support Office, a Detention Management Unit and an Ombudsperson's Office. The Public Information and Communication Unit is also part of this structure. Also, all these personnel are international and appointed by the same external organ, the Head of the EU Common Security and Defence Policy Mission, serving as the Head of the EULEX mission.

Articles 6,7, 8 and 9 of the Law No. 05/L-053 define the competence *ratione materiae*, *ratione temporis*, *ratione loci* and *ratione personae* of the KSC, that covers: international crimes, *i.e.* crimes against humanity and war crimes (more broadly, all criminal offences under international customary law applicable at the time the crimes were committed), those included in the 'CoE Report' and other crimes under the Kosovo Criminal Code (this is within the national aspects of the Court); offences that took place between 1 January 1998 and 31 December 2000; illicit conducts committed or commenced in the territory of Kosovo;[61] responsibility of natural people, that is nationals of Kosovo or the then FRY or individuals who committed crimes within the KSC competence *ratione materiae* against nationals of Kosovo or FRY, wherever those crimes were perpetrated and whatever is the feature of the armed conflict, national or international. Truly, the nature of the conflict that affected Kosovo is double: international, between NATO and the members states and Serbia; non-international, between the KLA and the Serbian

---

61   "Grave trans-boundary and international crimes committed during and in the aftermath of the conflict in Kosovo" and "which have been the subject of criminal investigation by the SITF", Law No. 05/L-053, Artt. 1.2, 6.1, 13, 14, 15.

Government.

The applicable law is: first of all, the Constitution of the Republic of Kosovo; customary international law and international human rights law, such as the European Convention of Human Rights and the International Covenant on Civil and Political Rights; the Law on the Specialist Chambers and the Specialist Prosecutor's Office; lastly, any other legal source of Kosovo expressly incorporated in the 'Law'. As subsidiary sources, the Chambers can refer to the jurisprudence of the International Criminal Court and other international criminal jurisdictions. While international law covers war crimes and crimes against humanity, Kosovo's domestic law covers ordinary crimes and criminal conducts.

Within the war crimes under investigation of the Specialist Prosecutor there are: murder, extermination, enslavement, deportation, imprisonment, torture, rape, sexual slavery, enforced prostitution, forced pregnancy and any other form of sexual violence, persecution on political, racial, ethnic or religious grounds, enforced disappearance of persons and other inhuman acts. No person will be tried before the the KSC for conducts that have already been tried by the ICTY or by any other court in Kosovo.

The KSC has the primacy over all other Kosovo courts and has the authority to order the transfer of proceedings from any other court in Kosovo to them. The same authority has the Specialist Prosecutor. The KSC has full legal personality, this means that, in order to fulfil their mandate, it can enter into international treaties with States, international organizations and other entities. It is located outside Kosovo, at The Hague, but has a seat in Kosovo. Amnesty or pardon cannot be called upon the KSC. Personnel of the KSC enjoys privileges and immunities accorded by the Kosovo law.

The Court has a financial autonomy from the Government of Kosovo, it is financed by the EU, but financial contributions can be provided also by third States. It became operational two years after the Assembly of Kosovo voted for its establishment, in June 2017.

6. The rationale for a mixed tribunal

Scholars contest that threats and incentives, a sort of "stick and carrot" tactic, were used by the UN and EU to exercise pressure on the Government of Kosovo. Some perceived the imposition of a new Court as an attempt to sovereignty of Kosovo. The pressures, indeed, would leverage a more widespread international recognition of the sovereignty of Kosovo as an independent State, its Euro-Atlantic integration and EU admission.[62] It was, furthermore, in question the conclusion of the Stabilization and Association Agreement between Kosovo and the EU.

This paper sustains that these undeniable external pressures have convinced the majority of the country that a special court inside Kosovo's jurisdiction would have been more suitable than a national tribunal or a completely international tribunal, potentially perceivable as excessively external to the nation. In fact, the proximity – not necessarily in geographical terms - is the sense of every mixed jurisdiction and in this case, the sense of ownership was promoted also by the circumstance that the KSC was voted by the National Assembly, not by isolated organs of the State but by the most representative institution, with the full support of the Government and of the President of the Republic of Kosovo. Thus, this Court has enjoyed the largest national support, if it is true that the vote of the Assembly was legitimate and nothing

---

62   *See* Heir, *supra* note 10, at 280, *"The KSL, as is clear, was established because of external pressure...The manner in which the KSC was established, and its related lack of legitimacy, thus poses potentially grave future problems for the KSC's proceeding's, and indeed societal stability in Kosovo."* and at 283, *"[...] the KSC was established by the Government and the Assembly of Kosovo because of external pressure, rather than in response to domestic support...this lack of public support constitutes a potential threat to peace and stability in Kosovo; [...]".* See also Muharremi, *supra* note 7 at 968, *"[...] the Specialist Chambers was imposed on Kosovo primarily by the EU using Kosovo's stabilization and association process with the EU as a political instrument to accept the creation of the Specialist Chambers.",* at 968.

lets to think the opposite. The political support cannot be denied because, even with the international pressure, the vote was not extorted. The KSC derives its legitimacy principally by the Kosovo Assembly, which voted for it. Detractors should criticize the Assembly that established the Court rather than the Court itself.

Some scholars discuss the legal classification of the KSC and its "regional" character, whereas they are compared with other tribunals acting in the field of international criminal justice.[63] Analysing their composition and jurisdiction, we can observe that the KSC is composed only by international judges and staff, because the letter of the President of Kosovo to the EU High Representative referred to "foreign staff only". Its composition convinced some doctrine that it is *only formally a Kosovo court and that it is in substance an international tribunal*.[64]

This assumption comes from the uncertainty in the literature that wraps the mixed tribunals, that do not always pay a single model, but that can embody different typologies.[65] They can be "nationalized" tribunals, international *ad hoc* tribunals but with some national elements (for example, when it is composed in prevalence by international judges and personnel but applies also national law)[66] or "internationalized", domestic in character but with some international features (for example, when it is part of the domestic judicial system, is composed in prevalence by national judges, but receives

---

63   *See* Cimiotta, *supra* note 8, at 57 et seq.
64   *See also* Muharremi, *supra* note 7, at 969.
65   *See generally* Dickinson Laura A., "The Promise of Hybrid Courts", in *AJIL* 97, 2003, at 295.
66   It is the case of the Special Court for Sierra Leone and the Special Tribunal for Lebanon. *See* Cataleta Maria Stefania, *Il Tribunale Speciale per il Libano*, Editoriale Scientifica, Napoli, 2014.

international assistance).[67]

The proximity coming from the mixed nature of the KSC, halfway between national and international dimensions, is an important factor in gaining national support. Mixed tribunals are generally located in the country where the crimes occurred, but not in all cases. The proximity suggests this geographical closeness, such as in the case of the Extraordinary Chambers in the Courts of Cambodia (hereinafter 'ECCC') and the Special Court for Sierra Leone (hereinafter 'SCSL'), but sometimes security reasons and fears of interferences discourage such nearness, like in the case of the STL, based in The Hague. Similarly happened to the SCSL, at the beginning located in Freetown, later displaced to The Hague in the case of Charles Taylor for security reasons. Thus, there is no univocity in this sense.[68]

The basic features of mixed tribunals are generally: the presence of national and international judges, prosecutors, lawyers and personnel; the application of a mixture of national and international law, according to international standards of fair trial and guaranties for the accused; the location, more often the *locus commissi delicti* or a more neutral *siège*. But, as stated above, mixed tribunals only in part share the same features, that is why it is relative and sometimes misleading reasoning just in analogical terms.[69]

According to *Muharremi*, in order to establish if a tribunal is mixed or international in character, one could apply the normative approach, in other

---

67   *See* Cimiotta, *supra* note 8.
68   *See generally* Donlon Fidelma, "Hybrid Tribunals", in Schabas, William A./Bernaz, Nadia, *Routledge Handbook of International Criminal Law*, 2011, at 85.; *See also* McAuliffe Padraig, "Hybrid Tribunals at Ten – How International Criminal Justice's Golden Child became an Orphan", in *Journal of International Law and International Relations* 7, 2011, at 151.
69   *See* Muharremi, *supra* note 7, at   990-991; *See also* Jain Neha, Conceptualizing Internationalization in Hybrid Criminal Courts", in *Singapore Year Book of International Law* 12, 2008, at 81 et seq.

words one should consider whether the court is a result of international law, such as international treaties or UN Security Council resolutions, or of national law, like in the case of the KSC.[70] If one applied such criteria it would result that the KSC is a mixed tribunal, more precisely an "internationalized" domestic jurisdiction, because the legal bases are the Constitution of the Republic of Kosovo and the 'Law' issued by the National Assembly, so both domestic law. Notwithstanding, the above-mentioned author concludes that it is an international tribunal "in substance" because of the composition of the panel, only international judges and staff, because of the total international financial support and foreign location.[71]

On the contrary, the present analysis maintains that the consideration of the panel and staff composition as the leading criteria to define the category of a tribunal is insufficient. The neutral location is demanded for security reasons, like in other similar tribunals of the same character, and the external financial support is just one within the international aspects. The main argument is that the Court is attached to the Kosovo judicial system, not just in a formal manner, even if it has the primacy on domestic courts. Given these mixed characteristics of the Chambers, in part domestic and in part international, other authors conclude that they *"cannot be perceived either as fully domestic or fully international criminal tribunals"*, but as a new category of regional criminal jurisdiction distinct from international criminal tribunals and mixed criminal tribunals.[72]

In fact, according to *Cimiotta*, mixed tribunals are the result of the interaction between the local governments and the UN, whose mixed tribunals would be

---

70   *See, e.g.* Muharremi, *id.*
71   *Id.*
72   *See* Cimiotta, *supre* note 8 at 59-69.

an extension in terms of post-conflict peace-building operation in the criminal and justice sectors, whereas in the case of the KSC there was no UN intervention but only from EU and CoE.

Furthermore, the difference between international criminal tribunals[73] and mixed criminal tribunals[74] is that the second ones are technically 'territorial based' (except for the STL and SCSL in the last period transferred to The Hague), belong to a State and operate within a domestic judicial system,[75] while the first ones *"act within the international legal order and under international law and, as such, their activity is not legally attributable to any state"*.[76] Given such distinction, the Chambers *"belong to Kosovo, to which their activity is formally referable. They are integrated into the existing structure of the justice system, operate within the existing domestic legal framework and act under Kosovo's sovereignty, as was held by the Constitutional Court in its judgement of April* 2015".[77] With this judgement, the Kosovo Constitutional Court confirmed the conformity of the creation of the KSC with Article 103(7) of the Kosovo Constitution.[78]

---

73   Namely: the ICC, the ICTY and ICTR.
74   Namely: the Special Panels for Serious Crimes in East Timor, the "Regulation 64" Panels in the courts of Kosovo under the United Nations Interim Administration of Kosovo (UNMIK), the Extraordinary Chambers in the Courts of Cambodia, the War Crimes Chambers of Bosnia and Herzegovina, the Special Court for Sierra Leone, the Special Tribunal for Lebanon and ultimately, the Special Criminal Chambers in Central African Republic.
75   The mixed tribunals would be the result of the United Nation's dissatisfaction with the two *ad hoc* Tribunals, due to the too log duration of the proceedings and the excessive costs, but especially due to the lack of domestic legitimacy and ownership of the trials; *see* Muharremi, *supra* note 7, at 969.
76   *See* Cimiotta, *supra* note 8 at. 61.
77   *Id.* at 64.
78   Constitutional Court of the Republic of Kosovo, judgement of 15 April 2015, Case No. K026/15. With this judgement the Court stated on the emendation of the Constitution with Art. 24 on the creation of the KSC, concluding that it would not have undermined any of the fundamental rights and freedoms guaranteed by the Constitution, available online at www.gjk-ks.org (accessed April 30, 2020).

The core element of a hybrid tribunal is to combine the form and substance of an international jurisdiction (with the subsequent international legitimacy), with the *"benefits of local prosecutions"* (with the subsequent national legitimacy),[79] because they generally operate within the jurisdiction where the crimes occurred.[80] This was the aim pursued in creating the KSC, whose potentiality was to fill the gaps present in the local judicial system and restore the rule of law.

These statements about international and domestic dimensions are used by the doctrine to attribute a regional feature to the KSC, due to Kosovo's obligation to comply with the EU obligations (elapsed with EU and the CoE). The Court would be the expression of an ongoing process of "regionalization" of the international criminal justice, due to the intervention and assistance of regional organizations.[81] In the same optic could be interpreted the creation, in 2012, of the Extraordinary African Chambers, by an agreement between the Republic of Senegal and the African Union, established within the Senegalese judicial system to prosecute the accused of international crimes committed in Chad between 1982 and 1990.[82]

Even the accuracy and word-reference of this theory, the author of the present work dissents from this perspective and maintains that the KSC is a new mixed criminal tribunal composed of both domestic (first of all the Court's inclusion in the Kosovo judicial system) and international features (first of all

---

79   *See generally* Nouwen Sarah M.H., "'Hybrid Courts' – The Hybrid Category of a New Type of International Crimes Courts", in *Utrecht Law Review* 2, 2006, at 191.
80   Office of the United Nations High Commissioner for Human Rights, Rule of Law Tools for Post-Conflict States – Maximizing the Legacy of Hybrid Courts, 2008, at 1.
81   *See, e.g.* Cimiotta, *supra* note 8 at 69-71.
82   *See* Adjovi Roland, "Introductory Note to the Agreement on the Establishment of the Extraordinary African Chambers within the Senegalese Judicial System between the Government of the Republic of Senegal and the African Union and the Statute of the Chambers", in *ILM* 52, 2013, at 1020.

the Court's international legal personality and powers in its relationship with other States in order to fulfil its mandate and the presence of foreign personnel). A discussion about what is for us a mixed tribunal goes beyond the purpose of this inquiry (the present analysis has only generally outlined the topic), moreover, this theory was useful to demonstrate the thesis of this work. Indeed, all the above-mentioned elements prove the existence of a link of proximity between Kosovo and the Court, that under these mixed features cannot be perceived as external to the country. This argument support again the opinion of the author about the full legitimacy of the KSC.

7. A new model of mixed tribunal

The assumption that the KSC is a new mixed tribunal comes from the main objectives pursued by every mixed tribunal: to protect certain interests related to the State, through their national features, and at the same time, protect interests common to the international community, through their international elements. The author considers that the UN intervention is not a necessary element to define a mixed tribunal and that this model of tribunals has suffered an evolution in the process of creation. This evolution justifies the involvement of other actors different from the UN, like in the case of the KSC. Mixed tribunals share similar objectives in States in post-conflict situations.

If one analyses the first mixed tribunals, like the SCSL and the ECCC, it is possible to observe both common and specific purposes. A common goal is the prosecution of military and political leaders responsible for gross violations of human rights and humanitarian law, that the national system has left unpunished.[83] Secondly, a common objective is to conduct independent and impartial trials guaranteed by the election of foreign judges. Another essential function is to fill up the gaps of the national judiciary system with a kind of justice more effective and respectful of international fair trial standards, in the case these are lacking.[84] This kind of tribunals are also capable to prevent corruption and political interference. Through this kind of justice, it is possible to contribute to the social pacification process and

---

83   *See generally* Edelenbos Carla, "Human Rights Violations: A Duty to Prosecute?", in *Leiden JIL,* 1991, at 5 et seq.
84   International standards conformed to the articles 9, 14 and 15 of the International Covenant on Civil and Political Rights and to the articles 5, 6 and 7 of the European Convention on Human Rights, concerning the rights of the accused and the criteria of a fair trial.

maintenance of peace in the country. In the two cases above mentioned, the UN intervention was coherent with the finality of maintaining the peace, because this is in the UN mission.

In the specific case of the KSC, the same mission is pursued at regional level, through the action of the EU and CoE.[85] The national reconciliation and maintenance of peace are sometimes preponderant elements and the judicial finality can be merely instrumental to the first elements, which are the goals pursued by the State concerned and by the international community.[86] This instrumentality would have been demonstrated by the failure of several mixed tribunals in judiciary terms, given the large number of serious gaps affecting the entire proceedings and the final judgements according to several criticisms towards mixed and international tribunals in the past. Their effective existence would have been more important than their real efficacy and functionality.[87]

In this case, the national interest is out of the question and the interest of the international community is carried out by regional institutions. The prevalent regional intervention does not exclude an international interest in the social pacification within the local community, coherently with the nation-building action in a region characterized by a strong ethnic fragmentation. After all, the international interest in the region is showed by the previous intervention of the UNMIK and establishment of the 'Regulation 64' Panels, the Bosnia-Herzegovina Chambers and principally the ICTY, antecedent to the KSC.[88]

---

85   *See* Williams Sarah, "The Specialist Chambers of Kosovo: The Limits of Internationalizations, in *Journal of International Criminal Justice* 14, 2016, at 25 et seq.
86   *See generally* Cimiotta Emanuele, *I Tribunali Penali Misti*, Cedam, 2009, at 431, 435 et seq.
87   *Id.* at 455.
88   The Regulation 64 Panels, formed by foreign staff elected by the UN, integrate the

The participation of regional actors, instead of the UN, in the creation of mixed tribunals (a function that is, furthermore, out from the Charter of San Francisco) is emblematic, showing the evolution of the international order and of the UN action, deferred sometimes to regional institutions acting with the same intent to preserve interest and values belonging to the whole international community and not only to the States individually.

Concerning the mixed tribunals, the values of the international community result from the combination between the duty to fight the impunity for *crimina juris gentium* and the maintenance of peace for States in transition. These values are the substrate for international security, even in the case of Kosovo where the creation of the KSC is the expression of a post-conflict peace-building activity so that the same atrocities will not occur again in the future. This post-conflict mission belongs not only to the UN but also to other international and regional actors particularly involved in a certain geographical area.

The international security is guaranteed by the removal of the causes at the origin of an armed conflict, by the resolution of local tensions, the attenuation of national instability and national reconciliation conforming to the rule of law. In this sense, we can speak of "interference" in the exercise of national functions linked to the judicial system. After all, this is the sense of a mixed tribunal (temporary in character but with permanent effects), that have mostly

national judicial organs in Kosovo and have competence on every crimes when there is a deficiency in the administration of justice at local level. While the Bosnia-Erzegovina Chambers, based in Sarajevo, have jurisdiction over the accused of medium rank in order to guarantee them the application of international standards of fair trial. They are a sort of extension of the ICTY, that has jurisdiction over the high rank accused. See Regulation of the UNMIK n. 9 of 15 May 2001, UNMIK/REG/2001/9 (*A Constitutional Framework for Provisional Self-Government in Kosovo*).

a preventive function in the interest of the international community.[89]

The typology of mixed tribunals is neither fixed nor uniform and is subject to continuous evolution and change, not necessarily degeneration. The KSC may be seen as the legacy of the ICTY but they actually express a new model of mixed tribunal.

---

[89]   See Cimiotta, *I Tribunali Penali Misti, supra* note 81 at 490, 529, 539.

8. The transitional justice process in Kosovo

"There is the national perception that the success of the institution will not necessarily entail a change in the national justice context of Kosovar society".[90] This perceived some commentators talking about the KSC, whose creation was accompanied by negative impressions at national level and enthusiastic sentiments at international level.

Three key principles support transitional justice: accountability, justice and reconciliation. The long-term aim of this kind of justice is to conduct post-conflict countries towards reconciliation and restore an effective and more robust domestic judicial system. At the core of this function there are the EU's four "essential elements of transitional justice", which are: criminal justice, truth, reparations and guarantees of non-recurrence/institutional reform.[91]

In order to ensure peace and stability, transitional justice guaranties justice for victims through the individuation of those responsible for past crimes and their punishment. Some people indicate such finality as a moral imperative.[92] The establishment of the judicial truth, trough a formal transitional justice process, is also important to dispel false myths and factious reality reconstructions susceptible to threat the stability in a region, like it has happened in the former Yugoslavia. In fact, the conflict in the 1990s was a direct result of the absence of a transitional justice process after the atrocities occurred during the Second World War, according to a certain narrative that

90   *See* Trigloso Andrea, "The Kosovo Specialist Chambers: In Need of Local Legitimacy", in *OpinioJuris*, 08 June 20, http://www.opiniojuris.org (accessed June 13, 2020).
91   *See* Heir Aidan, 'Step Towards Justice or Potential Time-bomb?', Report Kosovo Specialist Chambers, Balkan Investigative Reporting Network, Robert Bosh Stiftung, at 5.
92   *Id.* at 6.

focuses on the necessity to promote reflections on the origin of tragic events. Justice is the occasion to promote more objective reflections.

Criminal justice is only a part of the transitional process, that needs the support of national authorities and civil society, available to reconciliation. In this sense, national authorities play a crucial role in influencing civil society. A propaganda machine can condition public opinion negatively or positively. Thus, local ownership for transitional justice mechanisms needs political support in order to enjoy civil society support.

We can observe that the KSC lacks positive popularity because they are still a not well known institution and are at the beginning of their functioning. People did not have time to familiarize themselves. This may happen gradually after this new Court starts its mandate. It will achieve credibility if it works well. That is why it is still too early to stigmatize the Court now, as many political leaders do. Moreover, the lack of national consent in a part of the population is not sufficient to deprive this Court of legitimacy. Concerns about legitimacy stirred up the experience of several mixed tribunals, when the international assistance was firstly demanded by national governments (see the case of the ECCC and SCSL, but similar arguments concern the institution of ICTR as well) and later revoked (like the STL).

On closer inspection, the consent is not a presupposition for legitimacy to avoid the accusation of international interference in domestic affairs, having only the function to determine the modalities of the international intervention.[93] In this case, like the intervention of the UN in previous mixed tribunals, the EU and CoE have played a supporting role, assistance and

---

93   *See* Cimiotta, *I Tribunali Penali Misti*, *supra* note 86 at 523.

solidarity. This cannot be perceived as undue pressure. After all, the KSC was not imposed, like occurred in the case of the *ad hoc* Tribunals. These were imposed from the outside, through two UN Security Council resolutions, and were external to the national judicial system.

Some scholars sustain the thesis that this Court inherits the unfortunate legacy of the ICTY, that failed in the aim to promote reconciliation in the former Yugoslavia, feeding on the contrary a new wave of nationalism.[94] Within the causes there would have been the distance from the population, who have not understood the work of the Tribunal given also the bad outreach activity. Distrust against international tribunals perceived as an *extraneus* subject is common, but this does not necessarily mean that their action is ineffective or even counter-productive. The coercive force of a judgement is the same, both if it comes from a domestic tribunal and from an international one. In these arguments, the force of the law *per se* is contested and this cannot be permitted regarding serious violations of human rights. Moreover, an international tribunal is different from a truth and reconciliation commission, another transitional justice mechanism but with no coercive powers.

Many detractors are present within the former KLA commanders, now political leaders and members of the Government,[95] who do not support the KSC, who asked the revocation on some occasions. The idea to abolish the Court was also promoted by Ramush Haradinaj, Kosovo's Prime Minister, former leader of the KLA. On the other hand, President Hashim Thaçi, the

---

94   *See generally* Clark Janine Natalya , International Trials and Reconciliation: Assessing the Impact of the International Criminal Tribunal for the former Yugoslavia, Routledge, London, 2014, at 5.
95   Some political parties are the AAK, the NISMA and the PDK.

former political head of the KLA, affirmed that the decision to establish the Court was "unfair" and that he agreed with it at the beginning because he was *"under great pressure from the international community"*. The same Thaçi, during a press conference on the occasion of the 10th anniversary of the unilateral declaration of Kosovo's independence, sentenced: *"The Special Court cannot be abolished and will not be abolished, this is the attitude of the state, not an option"*.[96]

This confused and detrimental campaign affects the Court's ownership into the population and in this way, what that was created with favourable purposes for the Kosovo population becomes a hostile entity in the mass perception. It is evident that political legitimacy has repercussions over popular legitimacy, they are intimately linked by virtue by the propaganda machine. In this case, not the Court but the propaganda itself will impact negatively on the peace and stability in Kosovo.

Some criticisms throw fuel to the fire when stigmatize the prosecution against only KLA members by the KSC, which would make prosecution unfair;[97] in the collective imagination, they are seen as heroes in the liberation war against Milošević. The investigations concerning KLA members, however, do not discredit neither the entire movement nor the reconstruction of some events like History passed us. The Court duty is to establish some criminal responsibilities not to give a divergent lecture of the History, this remains primarily in the interpretation of historians, while the function of criminal proceedings remains restricted to determine the personal criminal

---

96   B92, 'Special Court for KLA "cannot be abolished" – Thaci', 1st February, 2018, https://.b92.net/eng/news/politics.php?yyyy=2018&mm=01&nav_id=103403 (accessed May 21, 2020).

97   *See* the study led by "Pax" conducted in 2017 in Kosovo on the public perception of the KSC, mentioned in Trigloso, *supra* note 90.

responsibility of specific individuals for specific facts. The History is not to be questioned but only criminal accountability.

This new transitional justice mechanism must contribute to inaugurate a new age not only in the inter-ethnic reconciliation between Serbs and Albanians within Kosovo, but also in the relations between Serbia and Kosovo, with an evident positive impact on the stability and peace in the whole region. This is the aim of transitional justice for post-conflict areas, whose process of transition and stabilization is activated also through the work of the international/internationalized criminal justice, one of the means to help such transitional process.[98]

Indeed, it is commonly agreed that criminal proceedings do not have just a legal value in the transitional justice process but furthermore contribute to re-establish and maintain peace in post-conflict countries, preventing the arising of new cycles of violence. The same CoE stated that there is no peace without justice for victims of past crimes,[99] otherwise the feeling of resentment will blow up one day in a new conflict.[100]

Justice has indeed the main role to clarify the truth, avoiding misrepresentations that can easily occur with the wrong interpretation of certain events of the past; justice prevents that the same errors happen again. According to this conception of transitional justice, a judicial mechanism must receive popular legitimacy, *i.e.* must be accepted by the population

---

98   *See generally* Murphy Coleen, *The Conceptual Foundation of Transitional Justice*, Cambridge University Press, Cambridge, 2017, at 1.
99   Council of European Union, 'EU's support to transitional justice', 13576/15, 16th November, 2015: 2, http://data.consilium.europa.eu/doc/document/ST-13576-2015-INIT/en/pdf (accessed April 22, 2020).
100   *See also* Subotić Jelena, *Hijacked Justice: Dealing with the Past in the Balkans*, Cornell University Press, New York, 2009, at 3-5.

concerned that has to show a certain confidence in its way to administrate justice.[101]

A study conducted in Kosovo explains the lack of local ownership of the KSC with four main arguments: international pressure was the main element supporting the creation of the Court; the persuasion that the previous judicial mechanisms, namely ICTY, UNMIK courts and EULEX failed to deliver justice and did not make the reconstruction of the Kosovar society; finally, the lack of support from Kosovar political authorities, showed by the circumstance that, in 2018, led to an attempt to abrogate the Law establishing the KSC.[102]

Indeed, we can distinguish between legitimacy, that regards the generalized appropriateness of an entity and its conformity to a system of norms, values, beliefs and local sense of ownership, that is the the sense of belonging and the popular acceptance of such entity. Now, concerning the creation phase of the KSC, there was acceptance by local authorities and popular representatives in Kosovo. There was also conformity to the law and a strong international legitimacy. Local ownership and the present absence of political support is a different question, not really well motivated because the work of the KSC, at this stage, cannot be still evaluated neither in a positive nor in a negative sense.

There is a diffused opinion that, when the creation of a jurisdiction does not have the local government's support, so it lacks legitimacy. This is not a valid argument to discredit a tribunal or frustrate its action. As maintained earlier, the creation of an international or mixed court comes from a mixture of an

---

101   *See* Murphy, *supra* note 98 at 122-123.
102   *See* Trigloso, *supra* note 90.

international and local impulse. Normally the *consensus* is not unanimous towards certain courts, not only at national level. The final results achieved through the trials are the test bench for these judicial organs, that is why sometimes only the time can confirm legitimacy.[103]

At the beginning of the functioning of an international tribunal, the presumed lack of legitimacy and legality are generally good arguments for the defence during the trial. The same arguments concern some predecessors of the KSC, like the ICTY, largely criticized as disconnected from the local community,[104] but whose work has finally been considered necessary in terms of transitional justice process, even in the international community perception.

Furthermore, the argument concerning the cultural and physical distance of these courts from the local population - see for example the ICTY, ICTR and STL (all located outside the country involved) - is feeble if compared with the need to protect victims during the proceedings and to prevent political interference and corruption, risks always present in States where the long-term reconstruction after a grave crisis makes the social and institutional order precarious and fragile. We can suppose that, in the case of Kosovo, it would have been uncertain the result of hypothetical domestic proceedings in terms of fairness, independence and impartiality.

Justice needs to be done and must be shown to be done, this is imperative for international criminal justice. A domestic jurisdiction cannot be the best solution because of its fragility about serious allegations. If one combine the

---

103   *See, e.g.* Hobbs Harry, "Hybrid Tribunals and the Composition of the Court: In Search of Sociological Legitimacy", in *Chi. J. Int'l L* 16, 2016, at 484.
104   *See generally* Fletcher Laurel E./Weinstein Harvey M., "A World unto Itself? The Application of Criminal Justice in the Former Yugoslavia", in Stover Eric/Weinstein Harvey M. (eds.), *My Neighbour, My Enemy,* Cambridge University Press, Cambridge, 2004, at 29-48.

fragility of a domestic justice system with a fragile State, like a country after a war, this can justify the preference for international criminal justice. In post-conflict regions, it is sometimes even arduous to investigate and even more to conduct a fair trial. That is why in certain circumstances an *ad hoc* tribunal is the most suitable solution also in order to guarantee the application of the best judicial standards.

Some argue that certain judgements, as the ICTY showed in the past, can exacerbate latent resentments, awake the buried lust of revenge, promote aggressiveness and cause inter-ethnic tension (in our case between Kosovo's Albanian and Serb communities), the same that gave origin to the conflict.[105] It is true sometimes, this could be a risk, but this argument cannot refrain from the necessity to prosecute certain crimes, otherwise, the real risk would be impunity. Furthermore, the failure to prosecute crimes committed during a conflict will mean a failure for transitional justice, which is a failure for the peace process. This combination of failures will not be an antidote against the commission of the same crimes in the future.

However, the present lack of popular ownership remains a pivotal problem, because people in Kosovo need to trust in a judicial mechanism created with the purpose to reaffirm the rights of victims that were violated during the war. This reaffirmation of rights through a reliable and trustworthy judicial organ can resolve the differences within Kosovar citizens, promoting at the same time reconciliation.

Wrongfully, the Court is compared to the ICTY and its supposed failure, as

---

105   *See* Heir, *supra* note 91, at 280; *see also* Subotić Jelena, "Legitimacy, Scope, and Conflicting Claims on the ICTY", *Journal of Human Rights,* 2014, at 172-175.

an *ad hoc* Tribunal created in New York by the Security Council and never accepted in the former Yugoslavia. But the KSC was created in Kosovo by Kosovo, conformingly to the Kosovar Constitution. If, on one hand, the formal and substantial legitimacy is a fact and cannot be denied *ab origine*, except for revocation, on the other, hand local ownership is not an irreversible condition. The KSC can still obtain popular support and produce a beneficial impact on the Kosovar community.

In order to pursue such finality, some measures are recommended by some authors, such as: extending of the KSC's mandate to also investigate Serbian attacks; inclusion of Kosovar staff and judges; overcoming the secrecy of proceedings, making them more accessible to the public in Kosovo; bridge-building through local initiatives and in this sense, the recent Draft Normative Act on the Truth and Reconciliation Commission of Kosovo can represent an opportunity to establish communication; finally, shifting the attention from the international community to the specific context of Kosovo, to have a real impact on the Kosovar society.[106] So, nothing definitive is still written for what concerns the KSC's role and operativity.

---

106   *See* Trigloso, *supra* note 90.

9. The necessity of public support

The sense of public ownership is not of secondary importance for an international tribunal, specially when it is located distantly from the affected country. Particularly, when these tribunals are based abroad, they are often perceived as alien; in such cases, it is necessary to establish communication between the tribunal, the victims and the community.

The proximity of the hybrid justice with the local population was for the first time promoted by the Security Council when it established the ICTY, located in The Hague. At that time the mission was accomplished also by an Outreach Program, fundamental to achieve the Tribunal's mandate. The program was to maintain a « *link between the work of the Tribunal and the people of the former Yugoslavia* », so that people in the region could share a *consensus* on the fact that the Court was legitimate. « *They must know, understand and appreciate the work of the Tribunal* ».[107]

The Outreach Program of the ICTY, launched in 1999, should face the misrepresentations and misunderstanding that affected the Tribunal in the local perception. The intentional propaganda instrument was increasing discontent within the different ethnic groups and this discredited the Tribunal.[108] The then President understood that it was essential for the process of legitimization of the Tribunal to convince the population that it had been created in their same interest. With this aim, some missions were organized in the country in order to meet the local actors and explain the role of the Tribunal and its independence and impartiality. Furthermore, the trials were

---

107   *See generally* McDonald Gabrielle Kirk, "Problems, obstacles and achievements of the ICTY", in *Journal of International Criminal Justice,* 2004, at 558-569.
108   *Id.*

transmitted online and the documents were translated in Serb, Bosnian and Croat languages.

This program was a trailblazer for the following international and hybrid tribunals and today all of these take care of an Outreach Program, that promotes also the public disclosure of the tribunal's activity, guaranties the publishing of information material and permits the visits of media and any other subject such as NGOs or schools. This informative action at local level should help primarily the reconciliation in the former Yugoslavia.

Unfortunately, in the case of the ICTY, differently from the following tribunals, the Outreach Program started quite late, six years after the beginning of its functioning and this made possible a persistent defamatory campaign by the local media and hostile politicians.[109] Today, such campaigns are more controlled concerning other judicial organs of the same character because the Outreach Programs start very soon, at the beginning of the tribunal's activity, but this has not eliminated the negative propaganda at all. In the case of KSC, non only the Court should engage in Outreach but also the Government of Kosovo in order to explain the working methods of the Court and bolster its local ownership.

Now, the contradictory behaviour of the Government of Kosovo does not justify the previous support and the present reluctance or hostility towards the KSC. The Government should explain the KSC to its citizens to promote local support. Such ambiguous approach of the Government risks causing inter-community tensions, civil unrest and political instability. Thus, it is the

---

109   *See generally* Orentlicher Diane F., *Shrinking the Space for Denial: the impact of ICTY in Serbia*, Open Society Justice Initiative, Open Society Institute, New York, 2008.

"establishment" and not the Court itself to produce negative repercussions in terms of transitional justice process. Similarly, a certain inactivity has characterized the Serbian authorities, that would have supported the KSC in Serbia as well.

Since the beginning of its activity, the KSC was engaged in an effective Outreach strategy, through the Public Information and Communication Unit, but also the Presidency and the Registry are very involved in communication activities. Public meetings and events are organized in the *siège* of the Court, in Kosovo and online through a YouTube channel. This activity is vital for the KSC that has faced with ominous omens concerning the impunity of the most prominent defendants, who would have received guaranties that they wont be prosecuted because only low-level figures and not the "big fishes" will be judged. According to this narrative, the Court would prosecute only direct perpetrators instead of the commanders.

In reality, this is not true. In fact, in June 2020, the Prosecutor announced he had filed a ten-count indictment charging President Hashim Thaçi, leader of the KLA between 1998 to 2000, along with Democratic Party of Kosovo chairman Kadri Veseli and nine others, with crimes including murder, persecution, forced disappearances, torture and other crimes allegedly committed against hundreds of victims, who were considered by the KLA as traitors of the independentist cause.[110] Following this announcement,

---

110   More in detail the indictment in the *Thaçi et al.* alleged that the accused were responsible as members of a joint criminal enterprise for the commission of crimes against humanity (persecution, imprisonment, other inhumane acts, torture, murder and enforced disappearances of persons) and war crimes (illegal or arbitrary arrest and detention, cruel treatments, torture and murder), including almost 100 murders. The indictment primarily focuses on crimes committed in Kosovo in the period prior and during the armed conflict. KSC, *Prosecutor v. Hashim Thaçi et al.*, Case No. KSC-BC-2020-06, Further Redacted Indictment, 4 November 2020.

President Thaçi withdrew his travel to Washington, accusing the KSC to want to rewrite the History.[111] Before the beginning of its function the defamatory campaign paints the Court as a corrupted political body colluded with the local "mafia".

Lastly, on 30 November 2020, the Pre-Trial Chamber of the KSC confirmed its first indictment,[112] where the Specialist Prosecutor's Office argued that the crimes were committed pursuant to a joint criminal enterprise (JCE). In confirming the indictment, the Chamber applied JCE in all forms, even if it seems that any reference to JCE is absent in the KSC's Statute nor in the Kosovo Criminal Procedure Code - particularly JCE III –[113] and it was not customary international law applicable at the time the crimes were committed. The confirmation decision reveals that there were public statements, publication and other readily accessible material that warned of, and/or encouraged the commission of the crimes alleged. As Pre-Trial Judge Nicolas Guillou found, the evidence establishes a well-grounded suspicion to satisfy an objective observer that Messrs. Hashim Thaçi, Kadri Veseli, Rexhep Selimi and Jakup Krasniqi committed the alleged crimes.

Many criticisms underline that it has taken nearly two-decade to initiate prosecutions for such systematic and widespread crimes of breathtaking proportions, with all the risks concerning the evidence, in many cases lost, compromised, or manipulated and after witnesses' memories has faded or influenced. 20 years after the commission of the alleged crimes are not a

---

111   Maupas Stéphanie, 'Le président du Kosovo accusé de crimes contre l'humanité', Le Monde, 24 July 2020.
112   KSC, Pre-Trial Judge, *Public Redacted Version of Decision on the Confirmation of the Indictment Against Hashim Thaçi, Kadri Veseli, Rexhep Selimi and Jakup Krasniqi*, KSC-BC-220-06, 26 October 2020.
113   *See* Articles 34 and 35 of the 2012 Kosovo Criminal Procedure Code, that not include JCE III. Furthermore, JCE's application to the alleged crimes committed from March 1998 through September 1999 would be *ex post facto*.

reasonable time, meaning to deny the accused expeditious proceeding. According to this arguments, it is fundamentally unfair to the accused waits until the evidence is uncertain, unavailable, untrustworthy. The same criticisms involve victims, because *justice delayed is justice denied.*[114]

For other opponents, the proceedings against the KLA heroic combatants would exacerbate societal anger, feed political instability, provoke new tensions between Albanian and Serb communities in Kosovo, cause a fresh outbreak of nationalism or Islamic fundamentalism and ultimately, worsening the Kosovo-Serbia dialogue. Furthermore, the new Court would be seen with disillusion by the Serb victims who have lost faith in judicial mechanisms after the failure of previous international and national judicial mechanisms.[115] To sum up, a catastrophic forecast accompanies the KSC at the beginning of its activity.

Scholars as well point out that judicial proceedings alone cannot achieve reconciliation, that relevant national authorities must support international jurisdictions and promote their legitimacy among the population and that, in any case, an international tribunal cannot work if it is externally imposed and managed.[116]

At the present, the KSC enjoys international support, particularly among EU, that has great expectations about their adequacy and appropriateness to pursue their purposes ; on the opposite, they suffer a lack of sufficient domestic support, specially among Kosovo's Albanian community, that

---

114   Karnavas Michael G., *JCE Redux – The KSC's first confirmed indictment (Part 1)*, International Criminal Law Blog, michaelgkarnavas.net/Blog.
115   From the "Pax study" in Trigloso, *supra* note 90.
116   Heir, "Step Towards Justice or Potential Timebomb?", *supra* note 91 at 17.

perceives them as an illegitimate foreign imposition and a body unfairly focused on Albanians.[117] The Court is perceived as a not necessary organ, whose working methods are unclear, having competence on crimes denied by the Albanian ethic group, who see the KLA accused leaders only as freedom fighters, refusing their classification as criminals.

Serbs in Kosovo support this new Court, but there is little consensus on its potential positive impact on the inter-ethnic relationship. In fact, many advocate the insurgency of new violence because such "illegitimate" organ would be an attempt to infringe Kosovo's sovereignty and Albanian's identity. According to these criticisms, it could offer a divergent historical reconstruction of the causes and accountabilities of the violence that occurred in the late 1990s.

Other opinions reveal disillusion : *"From the point of view of victim's community, there is no difference which Court is going to provide then justice. For them is important to see perpetrators to be convicted, it doesn't matter from which Court"* and concerning the historical reconstruction of atrocities of the Kosovo war, the KSC will prosecute only a limited number of cases, *"which are not enough to be basement for historical narrative".*[118]

There is a perception that the proceedings will not produce an effective result also because the trials will take place after more than twenty years and the witnesses will be inaccurate in their memories. Most of all, because of the endemic corruption largely diffused in Kosovo, there is the belief that witnesses will be intimidated and thus, forced to deny the allegations, as it

---

117   *Id.*
118   Personal interview with Amer Alija, Legal Analyst & Monitor of the Trials, Humanitarian Law Center Kosovo.

happened in analogous trials against KLA leaders before the ICTY. Finally, the Court is seen as an imposition in exchange to obtain Kosovo's international integration and such extortion would arise social anger, frustration, nationalist resentments intra and inter-ethnic tensions and hostility towards the international community.

Some concerns involve the security of witnesses, so that they feel encouraged to testify, as occurred on 14 January 2019, when the Court questioned Rrustem Mustafa, a former commander of the KLA. This aspect could fight the diffidence and insecurity of people. Within the main objectives of the KSC there is the capacity to fulfil the gaps and avoid the failures of the predecessor, the ICTY, in protecting witnesses. In that case, a big problem was to convince witnesses to testify, ensuring them from intimidations and interference. In fact, *"the reasons for establishing KSC are more related to the witness protection"* rather that the possible corruption in the domestic judicial system.[119]

In order to avoid and prevent any risks of intimidation and killing of witnesses, as occurred before the ICTY, the KSC have arranged a very serious and highly securitized protection program. There are rigorous measures to guarantee the safety of witnesses and victims, along with their physical and psychological well-being, dignity and privacy. They enjoy full privileges and immunities from legal proceedings concerning their statements and are not subjected to immigration restrictions for attending the Court's sessions. Many protective measures are ensured by the KSC, such as hiding their identity, giving testimony in private and closed Court sessions, and one-

---

119   Personal interview with Amer Alija, Legal Analyst & Monitor of the Trials, Humanitarian Law Center Kosovo.

way closed-circuit video links to keep the location of witness from being known.[120] The Rules of Procedure and Evidence provide that reasonable reparations are granted to victims from accused who have been declared guilty or has plead responsible for a crime which has directly resulted in harm to the victims.

Unfortunately, although these strict provisions and serious measures, in September 2020, thousands of alleged war crimes documents were taken away from the Office of Prosecutor and delivered anonymously to the KLA War Veterans' Organization. The files included the names of protected witnesses in cases at the KSC. The head of the War Veteran Organization, Hysni Gucati, claimed the files proved that the Specialist Chambers is biased against Kosovo Albanians and "established to fulfil Serbia's will".[121] This illegal action shows how the work of the KSC is hard in a so hostile climate of resentment, accusation and boycotts.

There is a debate on the future achievements of the Court. It is discussed if this Court will contribute to truth, justice and reconciliation, if the verdicts will be considered truthful and accepted by the public, if there will be public perception and understanding of the trials and if the Court's work will promote ethnic dialogue and mutual acceptance. All these factors will be verified once the Court will start judicial proceedings. At the moment, it is not possible a prognostic judgment or a *redde rationem* neither in a positive sense not in a negative one. It is not possible to forecast if the KSC will have

---

120   *See. e.g.* Crosby Alan/Zejneli Amra, 'Explainer: New Hague Tribunal Looks To Avoid Mistakes of Past Kosovar Prosecutions', *Radio Free Europe*, 18th January 2019, https://www.rferl.org/a/explainer-new-hague-tribunal-looks-to-avoid-mistakes-of-past-kosovo-prosecutions/29718149.html (accessed May 22, 2020).
121   Serbeze Haxhiaj, "Hague Prosecutors Take War Crime Case Files' from Kosovo Veterans", Balkan Transitional Justice, Pristina BIRN, 08 September 2020.

a positive or negative societal impact on Kosovo, that is why it is impossible to give neither a too optimistic nor a too catastrophic assessment.

However, some recommendations could be addressed to the Court, such as an always more effective Outreach Program, that needs to be conducted publicly and widely towards civil society in Kosovo, through public meetings and a connection with local media, with a permanent presence in Kosovo, through coordination with local civil society organizations and governments both in Kosovo and Serbia and through coordination with the analogous Outreach Government activity in Kosovo. Another important aspect is to maintain a strong cooperation between national and international judicial system.

In fact, *"the main risks between the KSC and the local judiciary may be the lack of serious cooperation between the two institutions; they need to work and help each other with mutual information or expertise and not to look themselves as two foreign institutions. For these 5 years of the existence of KSC we have not seen any joint conference of these two institutions except from a formal visit of KSC to Kosovo. From the work that is being done in the field and from the result that are seen in public, silently the local judiciary deals more with the crimes committed by the Serbian side and KSC deals with the crimes committed by the Albanian side. If there is no cooperation between the judiciary of Kosovo, Serbia and KSC in the mutual exchange of information and if this triangle does not cooperate then we will always have prolongation and obstruction of justice and each judiciary will be justified that the other party is not cooperating".*[122]

---

122   Personal interview with Amer Alija, Legal Analyst & Monitor of the Trials, Humanitarian Law Center Kosovo.

A suggestion for the Kosovar government, on the other hand, is to promote also truth and reconciliation initiatives in Kosovo, such as stimulating the inter-community dialogue on the past events and not entrust only to criminal justice the transitional justice process.[123] Furthermore, the negative press propaganda about the KSC should be transformed into a permanent favourable campaign. The Government should facilitate the cooperation with the KSC in order to deliver the Outreach Program, able to promote a complete understanding of the Court's function and work.

The government should fight misinformation and facilitate inter-ethnic dialogue. It should approach the society to the transitional justice process and conduct domestic courts to prosecute war crime authors. It should make easier the relations between Kosovo and Serbia. It should redouble efforts to promote inclusive truth-telling, civic commemoration and non-discriminatory reparations for all social categories, support local reconciliation initiatives. Kosovo's institutions should demonstrate political maturity by cooperating with the KSC and discouraging obstructionist responses.[124] It is important to combine the involvement of regional, international and local stakeholders in order to produce a positive impact of the KSC in terms of constructive societal changes.

The Government's support is fundamental also to influence the media that plays an important role, mainly because mass media are very politically polarised in Kosovo and mono-ethnic, often characterized by hate speech, misinformation and incitement of ethnic division.[125] The government must

---

123   *See* Heir, *supra* note 91 at 21.
124   *See* Visoka, *supra* note 42.
125   For a general overview, see the track record of proceedings in the Press Council of Kosovo: http://www.presscouncil-ks.org/. See also the Independent Media Commission:

mitigate all possible negative impacts and protect the KSC's reputation, explaining to the public the nature of the proceedings and the working methods of this Court. In this sense, it can be considered positively the Thaçi's decision to resign, on 5 November 2020, after the confirmations of the charges against him-self, to appear before the Court as a common citizen and not as President. This behaviour recognizes the legitimacy of the KSC.

The political support is the premise for the popular ownership attached to the KSC. This can facilitate reconciliation within intra-community and inter-community relations. If the Government wont work in this direction it will be the architect of the failure in the reconciliation process rather than the author of the failure of the KSC. *"The establishment of KSC gives a last hope to the families of the victims of all nationalities who have been victims of war crimes and crimes against humanity committed in the period 1998-2000 in the territory of Kosovo".*[126]

http://kpm-ks.org/?gjuha=3 and Una Hajdari, 'Kosovo Watchdog Condemns Threat to Journalist', BIRN, 9 July 2015, available at http://www.balkaninsight.com/en/article/kosovo-journalism-watchdog-condemns-veterans-threat-to-journalist (accessed June 19, 2020).
126   Personal interview with Amer Alija, Legal Analyst & Trial Monitor, Humanitarian Law Center Kosovo.

Part II

'When you know better, you can do better'. Some fair trial considerations on the procedural framework of the Kosovo Specialist Chambers

by

Chiara Loiero

1. Essential features of the procedural system

Kosovo Specialist Chambers are established 'within the Kosovo justice system'; Specialist Chambers are therefore attached to each level of the court system in Kosovo: the Basic Court of Pristina, the Court of Appeals, the Supreme Court and the Constitutional Court.[127] The Specialist Prosecutor's Office on the other hand has been constituted as a fully independent organ, mandated with conducting investigations and prosecutions without any interference from the Specialist Chambers, domestic Prosecutors, or any government or other source.

The procedure of adoption of the Rules of Procedure and Evidence arguably constitutes a special feature of the KSC. As it is common in international tribunals, the rules were first adopted by the plenary of judges. However, there are some remarkable novelties in the process of design and adoption of the rules followed in the context of the KSC.

The Law on Specialist Chambers and Specialist Prosecutor's Office (hereinafter "KSC Law") conferred to the plenary of judges the mandate to determine the Rules on procedure and Evidence (RPE); it stated that the rules were to reflect "the highest standards of international human rights law including the European Convention on Human Rights (ECHR) and the International Covenant on Civil and Political Rights (ICCPR) with a view to ensuring a fair and expeditious trial"; it further provided that judges, in

---

127   Art. 1(2) KSC Law; The Specialist Chamber of the Constitutional Court will only deal with constitutional referrals relating to the Specialist Chambers and Specialist Prosecutor's Office, and shall be the final authority for the interpretation of the Constitution as it relates to the subject matter jurisdiction and work of the Specialist Chambers and the Specialist Prosecutor's Office (Art. 49 KSC Law).

drafting the rules, were to be guided by the Kosovo Criminal Procedure Code of 2012 (which reformed the procedural framework in a more adversarial fashion).[128]

Of course, the drafters also had the benefit of the experience, case law and practice of the various international tribunals that have been operating over the last decades to draw and learn from.[129] Perhaps unsurprisingly therefore, the RPE present a high degree of similarity to that of other international or internationalised criminal institutions.

The vast majority of these tribunals have all followed in the path created by the drafters of the ICTY Statute, which set out to create from the synthesis between more adversarial and more inquisitorial models a new procedure that would allow the Tribunal to run fair and expeditious trials.[130] The result of this process is a hybrid legal system of international criminal law - a *sui generis* legal system of law and procedure comprised of a mix of Western civil and common law traditions and procedures, but significantly more adversarial in

---

128   Art. 19 KSC Law; Heinze Alexander, "The Kosovo Specialist Chambers' Rules of Procedure and Evidence: A Diamond Made Under Pressure?", *Journal of International Criminal Justice*, Vol. 15, Issue 5, 2017, at 8.

129   Sluiter Goran, "Human Rights in International Criminal Proceedings - The Impact of the Judgment of the Kosovo Specialist Chambers of 26 April 2017", *Amsterdam Law School Legal Studies Research Paper* No. 2019-23 at 27. KSC, Judgment on the Referral of the Rules of Procedure and Evidence Adopted by Plenary on 17 March 2017 to the Specialist Chamber of the Constitutional Court Pursuant to Article 19(5) of Law no. 05/L-053 on Specialist Chambers and Specialist Prosecutor's Office, 26 April 2017, KSC-CC-PR-2017-01 (hereinafter: Judgment on the referral), at 18: "*it seems that the Judges, in light of their background and expertise, have been borrowing from the procedural law and practice of various international and internationalized criminal tribunals as it existed in 2015, and which the judges deemed most suitable to ensure both an effective and fair functioning of the KSC*"; Heinze, *supra* note 127 at 8; Karnavas Michael G, "The Kosovo Specialist Chambers' Rules of Procedure and Evidence: More of the Same Hybridity with Added Prosecutorial Transparency", *International Criminal Law Review*, Vol. 20, Issue 1, 2020, at 89, 92.

130   Fiori Brando Matteo, "Disclosure of information in criminal proceedings: a comparative analysis of national and international criminal procedural systems and human rights law", PhD Thesis, University of Groningen, 2015, at 192.

its nature, which is adopted, with some variations, at the various ICL courts - except the Extraordinary Chambers in the Courts of Cambodia (ECCC).[131]

Because of the peculiar hybrid structure of the KSC highlighted above, the rules drafted by the judges had to be reviewed by the Constitutional Court of the Specialist Chambers and amended accordingly before entering into force. Upon review, the Constitutional Court found a number of draft rules (13 provisions in total) inconsistent with the Chapter II of the Kosovo Constitution (entitled 'fundamental rights and freedoms'); the judges revised the rules accordingly, and only after these amendments and their approval by the Constitutional Court, this time satisfied that they complied with Kosovo Constitution and international human rights standards, the rules were eventually adopted. In particular, the Court took issue with the lack of sufficient safeguards for the protection of individuals during investigations, as it will be further analysed below, and has importantly underlined the right to liberty, as well as making important remarks in regard to the 'principle of immediacy'.[132]

As it has been noted, the judicial - constitutional - review of the rules of procedure is a creative and commendable innovation that could be worth following by other courts in the future, given its potential to improve the legislative process and enhance the protection of human rights of individuals involved in criminal proceedings.[133] In this regard, it should also be noted that the Constitutional Court of the KSC has also a mandate to review any

---

131   Rohan, *supra* note 12 at 97, 99; Fiori, *supra* note 130 at 192. The ECCC applies a civil law system based on the French legal system; *see* also footnote 183 below.
132   Sluiter, *supra* note 129 at 27. Judgment on the referral, *supra* note 129 at para. 44.
133   Sluiter, *supra* note 129 at 19-20.

amendments to the RPEs to ensure their continued compliance with the Constitution of Kosovo.

Due to of all these circumstances, the procedural framework created by the KSC RPE provides for party-driven, adversarial proceedings with civil law-inspired procedural modalities;[134] the result is a body of rules that strongly resemble that of other international criminal tribunals, but includes in some of its parts more detailed provisions and additional human rights safeguards, arguably due to the explicit direction given by the KSC Law to the drafters of the rules towards ensuring the highest standards of fairness, and their subsequent constitutional review.

---

134   Karnavas, *supra* note 129 at 84.

SELECTED ISSUES AND RULES

2. Pre-Trial Phase: Investigations

As mentioned in Chapter 1, the procedural framework created by the KSC RPE is that of party-driven, adversarial proceedings; pre-trial investigations and information gathering are done entirely by the parties - there is no neutral investigative judge or prosecutor, unlike most civil law systems. [135]

The Prosecutor has the burden to prove the charges presented in the indictment. Investigations are initiated and led by the Specialist Prosecutor (SP), who will file an indictment if satisfied that there is a well-grounded suspicion that a suspect committed a crime within the jurisdiction of the Specialist Chambers; the Specialist Prosecutor and the SPO have the authority and responsibility to conduct investigations, and there is a police within the SPO at their disposal, with the authority to exercise powers given to the police under Kosovo law.[136] This is highly remarkable and a great advantage compared to the prosecutorial offices of other international tribunals who lack a police force and therefore have to exclusively rely on domestic cooperation.[137] This procedural phase is regulated in Chapter III of the Rules, dedicated to investigations and the relative powers conferred to the SP.

135
    Rohan, *supra* note 12 at 101.
136   Art. 35(3) KSC Law.
137   Heinze, *supra* note 128 at 6; see however Williams Sarah, "The Specialist Chambers of Kosovo: The Limits of Internationalization?", *Journal of International Criminal Justice*, Vol. 14, Issue 1, 2016, at 46, noting that cooperation will be essential, including for the gathering of evidence.

The section dedicated to investigative measures begins with two general safeguards, inserted following the Constitutional Court judgment; one is dedicated to the SP, and states that "during an investigation, the Specialist Prosecutor shall act at all times in a manner consistent with fundamental human rights";[138] the other one sets out some minimum safeguards that must be satisfied before investigative measures that may infringe upon fundamental human rights are authorised or undertaken (Rule 31).

Notable in this section is also the provision contained in Rule 32, which provides that material collected or seized as a result of any investigative measure that may be taken pursuant to Rule 34 to Rule 41 "shall be appropriately retained, stored and protected", and in particular that any decision by a Panel authorising such measures will include, *inter alia*, where applicable, the procedure for their preservation under Rule 71. It is indeed the latter rule that regulates specifically provisional measures that may be taken for the preservation of property and assets of the suspect or accused 'used for or deriving from the commission of a crime', following the issuance of an arrest order or arrest warrant or the confirmation of an indictment.

The effect of the Constitutional Court's judgment on the first referral is most tangible in relation to the rules regulating special investigative measures (Rules 34-36), for the definition of which Rule 2(1) refers to the Kosovo Criminal Procedure Code.[139]

---

138   Rule 30(2) KSC RPE.
139   These are: covert photographic or video surveillance; covert monitoring of conversations;

The Court in the judgment discussed these measures in detail, starting from the premise that each of the measures available to the Specialist Prosecutor interfere with a person's right to respect for privacy as protected by the Constitution as well as the ECHR, and that as such any interference can only be justified if it is in accordance with the law.[140]

Discussing the rules permitting covert interception of communications, and in regard to whether the interference is in accordance with the law and necessary, the Court found that rules 31-33 were not sufficiently detailed in regard to their duration,[141] the categories of persons in respect of whom the special investigative measures may be applied, and the conditions for their applications, especially for those involving a very high degree of interference with a person's rights. In sum, the Court found that the rules as formulated did not demonstrate to be kept to what is necessary, nor did they meet the necessary quality of law requirement, meaning that the law must be accessible and foreseeable in its application. The Court also found the draft rules permitting covert interception of communications to be lacking in the necessary specificity and therefore of adequate safeguards against abuse of power.[142]

---

search of postal items; interception of telecommunications and use of an International Mobile Service Identification "IMSI" Catcher; interception of communications by a computer network; controlled delivery of postal items; use of tracking or positioning devices; metering of telephone-calls; and disclosure of financial data, as defined in Articles 87(1)(1.1 to 1.7), (1.11 and 1.12), (2), (3), (4), (5), (6), (7), (11) and (12) of the Kosovo Criminal Procedure Code.

140   Meaning that it must be necessary for the fulfilment of its purpose in an open and democratic society; limited to the purposes for which it was provided; and not deny, in any way, the essence of the guaranteed right: Judgment on the referral, *supra* note 128 at para. 61.

141   *Ibid.*, para. 72.

142   *Ibid.*, para. 75

As currently in force, redrafted after the judgment, Rule 34 (Conditions for Undertaking Special Investigative Measures) specifies the nature of the offences which may legitimately give rise to the ordering or execution of special investigative measures, including interception orders, and the categories of persons in respect of whom special investigative measures may be ordered. Further, Rule 35, providing for special investigative measures authorised by a Panel, clearly sets out the conditions on which such measures will be authorised and conducted, in addition to clear limits on the duration of such measures.

Search and seizure measures are regulated in rules 37-39. The first provision regulates the authorization by a Panel of search and seizure measures requested by the Prosecutor, setting out the conditions at which the SP may request, and the Panel in turn authorize, such measures. Rule 38 also clearly defines the conditions under which the Specialist Prosecutor may carry out search and seizure without prior judicial authorisation, and requires the SP to consider the necessity of the operation.[143] This is another result of the Constitutional Court's judgment, which had raised doubts over the compliance of the relevant rule with Article 36.2 of the Constitution, which expressly provides that the authorities conduct searches only 'to the extent necessary' and where they are 'deemed necessary for the investigation of a crime'.[144]

---

143   The Specialist Prosecutor may, without an authorisation of a Panel, search a person or property, location, premises or object and temporarily seize items found during the search under the conditions specified in Rule 37(1) to (3), if: the person knowingly and voluntarily consents to the search and seizure; the person is caught in the act of committing a crime under the jurisdiction of the Specialist Chambers and is to be arrested after a hot pursuit; or it is necessary to avoid an imminent risk of serious and irreversible harm to other persons or property.

144   Judgment on the referral, *supra* note 128 at para. 86.

In regard to the legal framework governing the investigative phase of the proceedings, the RPEs of the KSC constitute a novelty insofar as they regulate a number of aspects of the measures that can be taken in this context, and particularly those more intrusive of individual rights. This is remarkable, and touches on an important point: when information gathering is done by the prosecutor, the important but limited role of judicial oversight in ensuring the protection of the rights of the suspects during the investigation stage of proceedings does not deny the need for strict and clearly defined rules in regard to investigative measures. And in most cases - this includes ICTY, ICTR and the ICC - these measures, including those infringing on individual rights, such as interception of telecommunications and search and seizure operations,[145] are not regulated in any detail. The absence of specific rules and the provision of judicial intervention can easily lead to extensive litigation in relation to the legality of the measures and/or the admissibility of evidence obtained in violation of human rights.[146]

This was well exemplified at the ICC by the *Bemba et al* case, where admissibility of certain items of evidence was a contested matter during trial. On

---

145   Sluiter, *supra* note 129 at 13.

146   Klamberg Mark, Evidence in International Criminal Trials: Confronting Legal Gaps and the Reconstruction of Disputed Events, Brill | Nijhoff, Leiden, 2013, at 223, citing Zahar Alexander & Sluiter Göran, International Criminal Law: A Critical Introduction, Oxford University Press, Oxford, 2008, at 367. See ICTY, Prosecutor v. Radoslav Brđanin, Trial Chamber Decision on the Defence "Objection to Intercept Evidence", 03 October 2003, IT-99-36-T, paras 61, 63(9), 355; see also ICTY, Prosecutor v. Momčilo Krajišnik, Trial Chamber Judgment, 27 September 2006, IT-00-39-T, para. 1189; ICTY, Prosecutor v. Zejnil Delalić et al, Trial Chamber Decision on the Tendering of Prosecution Exhibits 104–108, 9 February 1998, IT-96-21-T, para. 20; ICTY, Prosecutor v. Mladen Naletilić & Vinko Martinović, Appeals Chamber Judgment, 3 May 2006, IT-98-34-A.

appeal, the Appeals Chamber had to address the defence argument that the Western Union records presented by the prosecution as evidence of money transfers to witnesses were inadmissible because they had been obtained from Western Union in Austria in violation of the right to privacy.[147] While the majority eventually concluded that the interference with the right was proportionate to the investigative needs of the Prosecutor,[148] Judge Henderson, in a separate opinion to the judgment, criticised the hands-off approach of his colleagues and remarked the importance of judicial oversight "in situations where the Prosecution operates independently or national authorities are either unavailable or cannot be relied upon to genuinely safeguard the relevant human rights" and added that in such cases, the Prosecution has a duty to seek authorisation "for all investigatory acts that may infringe upon internationally recognised human rights".[149]

It seems safe to argue that if the ICC had a sufficiently comprehensive and detailed legal framework regulating the powers of the Prosecutor and the various investigative measures at their disposal, there would likely be no such extensive litigation on the admissibility of evidence allegedly obtained in violation of human rights and "all parties involved, including the Austrian authorities, could

---

147   ICC, Prosecutor v. Jean-Pierre Bemba Gombo, Aimé Kilolo Musamba, Jean-Jacques Mangenda Kabongo, Fidèle Babala Wandu and Narcisse Arido, Appeals Chamber Judgment on the appeals of Mr Jean-Pierre Bemba Gombo, Mr Aimé Kilolo Musamba, Mr Jean-Jacques Mangenda Kabongo, Mr Fidèle Babala Wandu and Mr Narcisse Arido against the decision of Trial Chamber VII entitled "Judgment pursuant to Article 74 of the Statute", 8 March 2018, ICC-01/05-01/13 A A2 A3 A4 A5, (hereinafter: Bemba et al. Judgment) paras. 218 and following.

148   Bemba et al. Judgment, supra note 147 at para. 336 and previous.

149   Bemba et al. Judgment, supra note 147, Separate Opinion of Judge Geoffrey Henderson, paras. 16, 17.

be reassured that an –invasive- investigative act/request coming from the ICC is in full conformity with human rights law".[150]

Indeed, lengthy and complex litigation can and often does occur when evidence requested by the prosecutor is collected by a domestic authority in order to then be transmitted to the international prosecutor; this may be linked for example to the way that this evidence is seized, handled, and stored before being transmitted and the lack of transparency that can surround such operations, which may affect not only the fairness of the investigative measure, but also cast doubt over its reliability for trial, with evident consequences in terms of length and efficiency of the proceedings. The approach adopted in international criminal procedure is to provide for the exclusion of evidence by judges only when the most serious breaches have occurred, and generally to admit any evidence that may have probative value, unless the admission of such evidence is outweighed by the need to ensure a fair trial.[151] In this sense, the advantage presented by the KSC framework in terms of clear rules (as well as a greater agency by the Prosecutor, which has a police force at disposal to carry out investigations) appears remarkable.

Furthermore, procedural legality is a requirement under human rights law for measures infringing on the rights of individuals,[152] and therefore the presence of

---

150   Sluiter, *supra* note 129 at 32; see also at 29, *"the manner in which investigations are regulated -or rather not regulated- at the ICC appears no longer to be in keeping with international human rights law, even if the impact of the KSC Judgement is taken at its lowest"; and at 32 "the implications of the KSC Judgement for the –investigative- law and practice of the ICC are potentially big and should lead [...] to significant law and policy changes at the ICC".*
151   Klamberg, *supra* note 146 at 396.
152   Sluiter, *supra* note 129 at 29-30; ECHR Article 8; European Court of Human Rights *Roman Zakharov v. Russia,* Grand Chamber Judgment, 4 December 2015, 47143/06, paras. 229-

rules in the KSC RPE attempting to regulate at least some aspects of invasive investigative measures and providing a role for judicial intervention in this context constitute an advancement in terms of procedural safeguards under international criminal law.[153] This is especially true following their revision ordered by the Constitutional Court, which, as detailed above, has led to a further improvement of the quality of the law to be applied to investigative measures.

Lastly, it is worth briefly mentioning the presence of rules explicitly regulating the storage and where applicable the preservation of seized assets, an important provision that should prevent the KSC from incurring the problems such as those arising at the ICC, where Jean Pierre Bemba, after his acquittal, filed a claim for compensation and damages partly based on the alleged negligence of the ICC in seizing and freezing his assets, as well as in managing them after their freezing.[154]

Overall, by regulating a number of aspects of the measures that can be taken during the investigative phase of the proceedings, the RPEs of the KSC constitute a welcome novelty, arguably raising the bar for procedural legality in international criminal law.[155]

238.

153   Sluiter, *supra* note 129 at 29.

154   ICC, *Prosecutor v. Jean-Pierre Bemba Gombo*, Public Redacted Version of 'Mr. Bemba's claim for compensation and damages', 11 March 2019, ICC-01/05-01/08-3673-Red, para. 6. The claim was ultimately rejected with the ICC, *Prosecutor v. Jean-Pierre Bemba Gombo*, Pre-Trial Chamber II Decision on Mr Bemba's claim for compensation and damages, 18 May 2020, ICC-01/05-01/08-3694. *See* Birkett Daley J, "Managing Frozen Assets at the International Criminal Court: The Fallout of the *Bemba* Acquittal", *Journal of International Criminal Justice*, Vol. 18, Issue 3, 2020 at 765-790.

155   Sluiter, *supra* note 129 at 32.

3. Arrest and Detention

Chapter 4 of the Rules is dedicated to Summonses, Arrest and Detention, and opens with the general provision that "No person under the authority of the Specialist Chambers shall be deprived of his or her liberty, except in accordance with the Law and the Rules"[156]. Pursuant to Rule 48(2), a Panel may issue such arrest warrants, summonses, decisions or orders "as may be necessary for the purposes of the investigation or for the preparation and conduct of the proceedings". Transfer from Kosovo or a Third State of the individual in question is addressed in Rule 50, while Rule 51 sets out a procedure for compensation for unlawful arrest or detention, which may be requested within six months of the decision.

Rule 52 and 53 address the different procedures to follow when a person is arrested depending on whether the arrest order was issued by the Specialist Prosecutor pursuant to Article 35(2)(h) or by the Panel.

When a person is arrested without an order by the Specialist Chamber, but rather upon issuance of an arrest order by the Specialist Prosecutor pursuant to Article 35(2)(h) and in compliance with 41(6) of the KSC Law, they must be brought in person before a Panel that will decide on their detention or release not later than forty-eight hours from the moment the detained person was brought before the court.

---

156   Rule 48(1) KSC RPE.

The Panel may also order the arrest and detention of a person when satisfied that the conditions for detention, set out in Article 41(6) of the KSC Law, are met: suspicion of commission of a crime under the KSC jurisdiction, coupled with 'articulable grounds to believe' that there is either a risk of flight, or a risk of obstruction of the proceedings by interfering with the evidence or witnesses, or a risk of repetition of the crime.[157]

The three individuals that currently held in detention in The Hague on behalf of the KSC at the time of writing have been arrested based on orders issued by a KSC judge.[158]

Particularly worth mentioning in this context are the provisions governing detention during trial. The KSC Law provides that a person deprived of liberty by or on behalf of the Specialist Chambers shall be entitled to a trial within a reasonable time or to release pending trial.[159] Further detail is found in the rules:

---

157   Art. 41(6) KSC Law: "The Specialist Chambers or the Specialist Prosecutor shall only order the arrest and detention of a person when:

    there is a grounded suspicion that he or she has committed a crime within the jurisdiction of the Specialist Chambers; and

    there are articulable grounds to believe that:

    there is a risk of flight;

    he or she will destroy, hide, change or forge evidence of a crime or specific circumstances indicate that he or she will obstruct the progress of the criminal proceedings by influencing witnesses, victims or accomplices; or the seriousness of the crime, or the manner or circumstances in which it was committed and his or her personal characteristics, past conduct, the environment and conditions in which he or she lives or other personal circumstances indicate a risk that he or she will repeat the criminal offence, complete an attempted crime or commit a crime which he or she has threatened to commit.

158   *See* KSC, Public Redacted Version of Arrest Warrant for Mr Salih Mustafa, 12 June 2020, KSC-BC-2020-05 (hereinafter Mustafa Arrest Warrant); KSC, Public Redacted Version of Corrected Version of Arrest Warrant for Nasim Haradinaj, 24 September 2020, KSC-BC-2018-01; KSC, Public Redacted Version of Arrest Warrant for Hysni Gucati, 25 September 2020, KSC-BC-2018-01.

159   Art. 41(5) 5 KSC Law.

Rule 57 provides that "the Panel shall ensure that a person is not detained for an unreasonable period prior to the opening of the case" and for the possibility of release under conditions in case of undue delay caused by the Specialist Prosecutor; it then provides for release of the detained person where sufficient grounds so require (meaning that the grounds permitting detention pursuant to Article 41(6) of the KSC Law no longer apply).

Rule 57(4) then deals with what happens when the release is ordered, and provides: "Upon request under paragraphs (2) or (3), the Panel may impose such conditions upon the release as deemed appropriate to ensure the presence of the Accused during proceedings, in accordance with Article 41(12) of the Law".[160] The Panel shall hear the Third State to which the detained person seeks to be released. A detained person shall not be released in the Third State without the consent of that State. A decision shall be rendered as soon as possible and no later than three (3) days from the last submission."

---

160   Article 41 KSC: "(…) 12. In addition to detention on remand, the following measures may be ordered by the Specialist Chambers to ensure the presence of the accused (including by video-teleconference "VTC") during proceedings, to prevent reoffending or to ensure successful conduct of criminal proceedings:

    a. Summons;
    b. Order for arrest;
    c. Bail with release in Kosovo, if the accused consents to attend proceedings by VTC;
    d. House Detention in Kosovo, if the accused consents to attend proceedings by VTC;
    e. Promise not to leave his or her place of current residence in Kosovo, if the accused consents to attend proceedings by VTC;
    f. Prohibition on approaching specific places or persons;
    g. Attendance at police station or other venue in Kosovo, if the accused consents to attend proceedings by VTC; and
    h. Diversion.

Comparison with other tribunals and fair trial considerations

In the first edition of the rules of the *ad hocs*, judges were only permitted to grant provisional release to those awaiting trial 'in exceptional circumstances'. This choice was strongly criticised and the rules later amended to provide that release may be ordered during trial; however this may only occur after giving the host country and the State to which the accused seeks to be released the opportunity to be heard and only if the Chamber is satisfied that the accused will appear for trial and, if released, will not pose a danger to any victim, witness or other person.[161]

At the ICC on the other hand, the Pre-Trial chamber *shall* release the person if the conditions that justified the arrest are no longer met, meaning that is under a positive obligation to do so.[162] It is worth noting that at the ICC, these conditions include the need to ensure the presence of the accused at trial. Differently phrased, Rule 57 KSC RPE states that a Panel *may* release the detained person where sufficient grounds require the release of the detained person. The need to ensure the presence of the accused at trial however is not one of the grounds justifying detention *per* Article 41(6) KSC Law. In this regard, as seen above, Rule 57(4) provides that the Panel may impose conditions upon release as deemed appropriate to ensure the presence of the accused during proceedings, in accordance with Article 41(12) of the Law.

---

161   McDermott *supra* note 14 at 81 and fn. 16. Rules 65(B) ICTY, ICTR and Rule 68(B) IRMCT.
162   Article 58(1)(b) ICC Rome Statute; McDermott *supra* note 14 at 82.

The second part of the same Rule 57(4) had to be amended after the judgment by the Constitutional Court. In reviewing the draft rule, the Court took issue with the way the provision was formulated ("A detained person shall not be released without the consent of that State"), finding that the plain meaning of the text of that provision made the release of a detained person entirely dependent upon the consent of the Third State even where the person's release was required. This, according to the Court, would be 'inconceivable in a State subject to the rule of law'; it would render any detention lacking the necessary legal basis and therefore unlawful, which rendered the provision contrary to the Constitution and human rights law.[163] Upon referral of the revised rules, the Court was satisfied with the slight amendment made to Rule 57(4) ["A detained person shall not be released *__in the Third State__* without the consent of that State" (emphasis added)].

While it goes beyond the present contribution to discuss the broader issue of the deprivation of liberty of accused individuals during trial - undoubtedly one of the main human rights issues in the context of international criminal justice,[164] the importance of the pronouncement of the Constitutional Court that it is a violation of the right to liberty to make provisional release of a suspect dependent upon the cooperation of a State should not be understated.[165] This pronouncement is surely in compliance with human rights, and it is in direct contradiction with the case law of the ICC, where the ICC Appeals Chamber

---

163   Judgment on the referral, *supra* note 128 at para. 120.
164   Rearick Daniel J, "Innocent Until Alleged Guilty: Provisional Release in the ICTR", *Harvard International Law Review* Vol. 44, Issue 2, 2003, 577-596; Doran Kate, "Provisional Release in International Human Rights Law and International Criminal Law", *International Criminal Law Review*, Vol. 11, Issue 4, 2011, 707–743.
165   Sluiter, *supra* note 129 at 27.

ruled that release was conditional upon the willingness of a State willing to accept the person to be released.[166]

It should also be added that, differently from other international criminal tribunals, the KSC legal framework provides some guidance on provisional release; the Kosovo Specialist Chambers' Headquarters agreement with the Netherlands specifically states that persons shall not be provisionally released in the Host State,[167] and the KSC further provides that, when release is ordered for a person detained in the host state, the detainee shall not be released there, but instead transported either to where they were originally detained on the KSC's behalf, to a place where they are ordinarily and lawfully resident, or to another state that agrees to accept them.[168]

In brief, the effective enjoyment of the right to liberty when provisional release of an accused is granted will still be dependent on the availability of any the options foreseen by the law.

---

166 Sluiter, *supra* note 129 at 28; ICC, *Prosecutor v. Jean-Pierre Bemba Gombo,* Appeals Chamber Judgement on the appeal of the Prosecutor against Pre-Trial Chamber II's "Decision on the Interim Release of Jean-Pierre Bemba Gombo and Convening Hearings with the Kingdom of Belgium, the Republic of Portugal, the Republic of France, the Federal Republic of Germany, the Italian Republic, and the Republic of South Africa", 02 December 2009, ICC-01/05/01-08 OA 2, para. 106; International Bar Association, "Provisional release, release at advanced stages of proceedings, and final release at international criminal courts and tribunals", *ICC & ICL Programme Discussion Paper Series*, October 2019, 11-12.
167 Agreement between the Kingdom of the Netherlands and the Republic of Kosovo concerning the Hosting of the Kosovo Relocated Specialist Judicial Institution in the Netherlands, Art 42.
168 Art. 41(11) KSC Law. See International Bar Association *supra* note 157.

4. Indictment

Upon a well-grounded suspicion that a suspect committed a crime within the jurisdiction of the Specialist Chambers, the Specialist Prosecutor may file before a Pre-Trial Judge an indictment together with its supporting material (Rule 86).

If an indictment is not filed within a reasonable time after the person became a suspect, the suspect may request the Specialist Prosecutor to terminate the investigation against him or her.[169]

When an indictment is filed, it is reviewed by a Pre-Trial Judge, that shall confirm the indictment if satisfied that a well-grounded suspicion has been established, or dismiss the indictment if not; in that case however, the Prosecutor is not precluded from subsequently requesting the confirmation of the indictment if the request is supported by additional evidence. Rule 85(5) directs the Pre-Trial Judge to set a target date for the decision "which, subject to the specificities of the case, shall be no later than six (6) months from the filing of the indictment and all supporting material".

If the indictment is confirmed, the judge may issue any order and warrants for the arrest and transfer of the person (or persons) in question.

Rule 86(3)(b) specifies that the indictment shall include "a detailed outline demonstrating the relevance of each item of evidentiary material to each

---

169   Rule 47 KSC RPE.

allegation, with particular reference to the conduct of the suspect with respect to the alleged crime".

Rule 90 allows the Prosecutor to amend the indictment up until trial proceedings, with modalities that appears modelled after the amendment/withdrawal of charges at the ICC;[170] the Prosecutor may amend the indictment at any time without leave, before its confirmation, and with leave of the Pre-Trial Judge who confirmed the indictment, between the confirmation and the assignment of the case to the Trial Panel, or, after assignment of the case to the Trial Panel, with leave of that Panel.[171]

Comparison with other tribunals and fair trial considerations

While the rules on the indictment strongly resemble those of the ICTY-ICTR, the KSC rules present at least one remarkable feature: the level of detail required from the Prosecutor in the indictment, and the specific obligation to include the provision of a detailed analysis of the evidence as related to the specific charges (Rule 86(3)(b)); a 'far reaching obligation" imposed on the SP, according to one commentator.[172] No such provision exists in other international criminal tribunals, where the relative rules require much lower level of detail in the indictment.[173] At the same time, there have been many instances in which such an

---

170   Heinze, *supra* note 128 at 9.
171   Some warned that this may lead to delays in the proceedings; see Heinze, *supra* note 127 at 10, citing Karnavas *supra* note 129.
172   Heinze, *supra* note 128 at 10.
173   Rule 47(B) ICTY/ICTR RPE; Rule 68(B) STL RPE. See also Rule 47(C) SCSL RPE and S. 24 Regulation 2000/30 of the Special Panels for Serious Crime in East Timor. At the ICC, the term 'indictment' is not used, the Prosecutor applies for a warrant of arrest, see Rome Statute Art. 58(2). See ICTY, *Prosecutor v. Blagoje Simić*, Appeals Chamber Judgement, 28 November 2006,

effort in detailing the charges has been specifically required from the Prosecutor; at the ICC for example, several chambers have required the filing of an "in-depth analysis chart",[174] ("an auxiliary document next to the document containing the charges and the list of evidence")[175] which, while more strictly linked with the disclosure obligations imposed on the Prosecutor (see next paragraph) is aimed at achieving something similar to what Rule 86(3)(b) KSC requires at the indictment stage.[176]

Specificity of the charges is key to compliance with an individual's right to be properly informed of their charges,[177] and rules on the formulation of the

---

IT-95-9-A, at para. 20 (hereinafter *Simić* Appeal Judgment); ICTY, *Prosecutor v. Jadranko Prlić et al.*, Appeals Chamber Judgement, 29 November 2017, IT-04-74-A, at para. 27.

174   ICC, *Prosecutor v. Jean-Pierre Bemba Gombo*, Pre-Trial Chamber III Decision on the Submission of an Updated, Consolidated Version of the In-depth Analysis Chart of Incriminatory Evidence, 10 November 2008, ICC-01/05-01/08-232, paras. 6–9; ICC, *Prosecutor v. Dominic Ongwen*, Pre-Trial Chamber II Decision Setting the Regime for Evidence Disclosure and Other Related Matters, 27 February 2015, ICC-02/04-01/15-203, paras. 38–39 (hereinafter, *Ongwen* Disclosure Decision). See however ICC, *Chambers Practice Manual*, 2019, at 6, 11 "*no submission of any 'in-depth analysis chart', or similia, (...) can be imposed on either of the parties*".

175   *Ongwen* Disclosure Decision, para. 39.

176   Heinze, *supra* note 128 at 94.

177   ICC Statute, art. 55(2)(a), art. 67(1)(a), Rule 121(3), and Rule 122(1); ICTY Statute, art. 21(4)(a); ICTR Statute, art. 20(4)(a); see MICT, *Prosecutor v, Maximilien Turinabo et al*, Single Judge Decision on Dick Prudence Munyeshuli's Motion Alleging Defects in the Indictment, 12 March 2019, MICT-18-116-PT, at para. 5 62; *Prosecutor v. Jovica Stanišić & Franko Simatović*, Trial Chamber Decision on Prosecution Motion for Reconsideration and Further Submission, 11 February 2019, MICT-15-96-T, at para. 10 63 (hereinafter, *Stanišić* Reconsideration Decision); MICT, *Augustin Ngirabatware v. Prosecutor*, Appeals Chamber Judgement, 18 December 2014, MICT-12-29-A, at para. 32 (hereinafter, *Ngirabatware* Appeal Judgment); MICT, *Prosecutor v. Jovica Stanišić & Franko Simatović*, Trial Chamber Decision on Stanisic's Motion for Further Particularisation of the Prosecution's Case, 2 May 2018, MICT-15-96-T, at para. 11 (hereinafter, *Stanišić* Decision on Further Particularisation); ICC *Prosecutor v. Lubanga*, Judgment on the appeal of Mr Thomas Lubanga Dyilo against his conviction, 1 December 2014; *Prosecutor v. Yekatom*, Pre-Trial Chamber Decision on the Confirmation of Charges against Alfred Yekatom and Patrice Edouard Ngaissona, 11 December 2019, para. 28; *Prosecutor v. Ongwen*, Appeals Chamber Judgment on the Appeal of Mr. Dominic Ongwen Against Trial Chamber IX's Decision on Defence Motions Alleging Defects in the Confirmation Decision, 17 December 2019, para. 69.

indictment are highly relevant for the protection of fair trial rights.[178] Having a detailed outline of the allegations and how the evidence presented supports them can provide the defence with adequate notice of the charges and a clear understanding of the prosecution's case going into trial, which is especially useful considered the limited time and resources (especially if indigent) at the disposal of an accused.[179]

Chambers have on occasions reaffirmed the right of the accused person to be informed of the charges[180] and the "strong link between the right to be informed in detail of the nature, cause and content of the charges and the right to prepare one's defence".[181]

The greater specificity required from the Prosecutor at the indictment stage can also be particularly useful for the pre-trial Judge in making the determination whether to confirm the indictment, and is therefore seen as promoting efficiency and expeditiousness of trials, in addition to fairness.[182]

---

178   McDermott *supra* note 14 at 28.
179   Karnavas *supra* note 129 at 100.
180   *Simić* Appeal Judgment at para. 20; ICTR, *Georges Anderson Nderubumwe Rutaganda v. Prosecutor*, Appeals Chamber Judgement, 26 May 2003, ICTR-96-3-A, at para. 303; ICTR, *Prosecutor v. André Ntagerura et al*, Appeals Chamber Judgement, 7 July 2006, ICTR-99-46-A, at para. 121; ICTR, *Ferdinand Nahimana et al v. Prosecutor*, Appeals Chamber Judgment, 28 November 2007, ICTR-99-52-A, at para. 322; *Stanišić* Reconsideration Decision, at para. 10 63; *Ngirabatware* Appeal Judgment at para. 32; *Stanišić* Decision on Further Particularisation at para. 11.
181   ICC, *Prosecutor v. Dominic Ongwen*, Appeals Chamber Judgment on the Appeal of Mr. Dominic Ongwen Against Trial Chamber IX's 'Decision on Defence Motions Alleging Defects in the Confirmation Decision', 17 July 2019, ICC-02/04-01/15-1562, at para. 69.
182   ICC, *Prosecutor v. Dominic Ongwen*, Appeals Chamber Judgment on the Appeal of the Prosecutor the decision of Pre-Trial Chamber II entitled "Decision Setting the Regime for Evidence Disclosure and Other Related Matters", 17 June 2015, ICC-02/04-01/15-251, at paras. 42-43; ICC, *Prosecutor v. Al Hassan Ag Abdoul Aziz Ag Mohamed Ag Mahmoud*, Pre-Trial Chamber I Decision on the In-Depth Analysis Chart of Disclosed Evidence, 29 June 2018, ICC-01/12-01/18-61-tENG,

The KSC RPE in this respect therefore constitute a novel and arguably commendable effort in regulating the manner in which the Prosecutor is bound to discharge the burden of proof at the pre-trial stage while seeking to promote efficiency and fairness of the proceedings.

At the time of writing, the SPO has filed at least two indictments, one of which has been confirmed by a KSC judge in four months.[183]

---

at para. 22; ICC, *Prosecutor v. Alfred Yekatom and Patrice-Edouard Ngaïssona*, Pre-Trial Chamber II Second Decision on Disclosure and Related Matters, 4 April 2019, ICC-01/14-01/18-163, at para. 24. See however Heinze, *supra* note 129 warning that requiring an in-depth analysis chart has been occasionally seen as a potential cause for delay of proceedings, and that it bears considerable risks, including '*aggravating the conflict of legal traditions*' by requiring the Prosecutor to disclose parts of their legal analysis and putting the Pre-Trial Judge into an even more active role before trial (a rather uncommon feature in adversarial proceedings), as well as the need for more resources.

183   See Mustafa Arrest Warrant, *supra* note 15; pursuant to Rule 88(2) of the Rules of Procedure and Evidence Before the Kosovo Specialist Chambers the indictment, as confirmed, was not made public at that time.

5. Disclosure of Evidence by the Prosecutor

A key component of the adversarial form of international criminal proceedings[184] and of the prosecutorial obligations towards the defence is disclosure of evidence, which goes to supplement the right of the accused to be informed promptly of the charges, and is therefore an essential element of the right to a fair trial.[185]

The KSC RPE, as did the *ad hoc* tribunals and the Special Court for Sierra Leone (SCSL), have followed the common law model with rather complex rules on disclosure,[186] to which an entire chapter is dedicated, consisting of 10 rules.[187]

The KSC RPE contain rules regulating disclosure by the specialist prosecutor and by the defence (rules 102 and 104), and disclosure of exculpatory evidence, which shall be disclosed "immediately" to the defence (Rule 103). Material supporting the indictment and statements obtained from the accused must be disclosed as soon as possible, but at least within thirty days of the initial

---

184   Klamberg, *supra* note 146 at 844; but see McDermott *supra* note 14 at 122: "*the prosecutorial disclosure obligation cannot be slotted neatly along the adversarial/inquisitorial spectrum, and has been described as 'an inquisitorial modification of a pure adversary system '*".
185   Kaoutzanis Christodoulos, "A Turbulent Adolescence Ahead: The ICC's Insistence on Disclosure in the Lubanga Trial", *Washington University Global Studies Law Review*, Vol. 12, Issue 2, 2013, at 270, citing Swoboda Sabine, "The ICC Disclosure Regime—A Defence Perspective", *Criminal Law Forum*, Vol. 19, Issue 3, 2008, at 449, 450; Ambos Kai, "Confidential Investigations (Article 54(3)(E) ICC Statute) vs. Disclosure Obligations: The Lubanga Case and National Law", *New Criminal Law Review*, Vol. 12, Issue 4, 2009, at 543, 547.
186   Klamberg, *supra* note 146 at 274; Tochilovsky Vladimir, *Jurisprudence of the International Criminal Courts and the European Court of Human Rights,* Brill | Nijhoff, Leiden, at 95 See ICTY, ICTR and SCSL Rules 66–68 and MICT Rules 71–73.
187   Heinze, *supra* note 129 at 9.

appearance of the accused, while the rest of the material[188] shall in any case be disclosed no later than thirty days prior to the opening of the Specialist Prosecutor's case.

*

While the RPE do not specify that the disclosure obligations of parties include information as to the identities of the witnesses in addition to their statements, this can arguably be considered to be implied. This appears to be confirmed by Rule 105 ('Interim Non-Disclosure of Identity'), which provides that "in exceptional circumstances, the Parties (…) may apply to the Panel for interim non-disclosure of the identity of a witness or a victim participating in the proceedings at risk until appropriate protective measures have been ordered".

Paragraph 3 of Rule 105 specifies that "the identity of the witness shall be disclosed sufficiently in advance in order to allow for the preparation of the defence"; however this is "subject to Rule 80(4)(e)", which in turn provides that, pursuant to an order by the Panel for the protection of witnesses, measures ordered may include, "in exceptional circumstances, and subject to any necessary safeguards: (i) non-disclosure to the Parties of any material or information that may lead to the disclosure of the identity of a witness or victim participating in the proceedings; or (ii) total anonymity of a witness." It is therefore possible that the identity of one or more witnesses may never be

---

188   These are: (i) the statements of all witnesses whom the Specialist Prosecutor intends to call to testify at trial; (ii) all other witness statements, expert reports, depositions, or transcripts that the Specialist Prosecutor intends to present at trial; (iii) the statements of additional Specialist Prosecutor witnesses upon the decision to call those witnesses; and (iv) the exhibits that the Specialist Prosecutor intends to present at trial.

disclosed to the defence. Rule 80(1) specifies that any of the listed measures may be ordered 'provided that the measures are consistent with the rights of the accused'.

*

The RPE also contain provisions regarding protected information not subject to disclosure; the first deals with information not subject to disclosure because provided on a confidential basis, and therefore protected under Article 58 of the KSC Law. Rule 107 expressly provides in relation to information in control of the Specialist Prosecutor "which has been provided on a confidential basis and solely for the purpose of generating new evidence" that the initial material or information "shall, in any event, not be tendered into evidence without prior disclosure to the Accused." The rule directs the Specialist Prosecutor, where the information is subject to disclosure, to provide the information and apply *ex parte* to the Panel for a determination over their obligation under Rule 102 and Rule 103 to disclose the initial material; the Specialist Prosecutor may also apply for counterbalancing measures pursuant to Rule 108.[189] If consent is obtained from the provider of the initial material and the Specialist Prosecutor chooses to present any of it as evidence, Rule 107(5) safeguards the right of the accused to challenge the evidence presented by the Specialist Prosecutor, albeit subject to the limitations contained in paragraphs (3) and (4); limitations that, however, shall not "affect the power of the Panel to exclude this evidence or to

---

189   *See* fn. 190 below.

106

take any measures necessary to ensure the fairness of the proceedings" (Rule 107(7)).

Further, Rule 108 ('Other Information Not Subject to Disclosure') deals with information in control or knowledge of the Specialist Prosecutor that is subject to disclosure under Rule 102 or Rule 103, but that the Specialist Prosecutor believes to have reasons not to disclose.[190]

When making an application to the Panel to withhold the information in whole or in part, the Specialist Prosecutor shall include "the information in question, the reasons for non-disclosure, the proposed redactions, if any, and a statement relating to the proposed counterbalancing measures" (Rule 108(2)).[191] The Panel will then decide first whether the information is subject to disclosure, and where it finds that this is the case, it will consider the Specialist Prosecutor's reasons for non-disclosure and the counterbalancing measures proposed (Rule 108(2)). Rule 108(4) importantly provides that, if the Panel considers that no measures would ensure the accused's right to a fair trial, the Specialist Prosecutor shall be

---

190   Rule 108(1): "Where information in the custody, control or actual knowledge of the Specialist Prosecutor is subject to disclosure under Rule 102 or Rule 103, but such disclosure may:
        prejudice ongoing or future investigations;
        cause grave risk to the security of a witness, victim participating in the proceedings or members of his or her family; or
        be contrary for any other reason to the public interest or the rights of third parties;
    the Specialist Prosecutor may apply confidentially and ex parte to the Panel to withhold the information in whole or in part.
191   These may include:
        identification of new, similar information;
        submission of a summary of the information;
        submission of the information in a redacted form; or
        stipulation of the relevant facts regarding the reasons for non-disclosure.

given the option of either disclosing the information, or amending or withdrawing the charges to which the information relates.

*

Another provision to point out, arguably the most notable feature in this chapter of the RPE is Rule 110; dealing with 'Non-Compliance with Disclosure Obligations'. The rule states that a panel of judges may decide (upon request or on its own initiative) on measures to be taken as a result of the non-compliance with disclosure obligations, *including a stay of proceedings and the exclusion of evidence* (Rule 110) (emphasis added).

Comparison with other tribunals and fair trial considerations

As mentioned above, The KSC RPE follow the common law model with rather complex rules on disclosure, as did the *ad hoc* tribunals and others. [192] However, while the KSC rules on disclosure follow a substantially similar structure to the ones of other international criminal tribunals, they differ in some important details. For example, the KSC RPE are noteworthy in how they regulate the matter of evidence obtained by the Prosecutor protected by confidentiality; Rule 107 strongly resembles the correspondent ICC and ICTY rules insofar as it clarifies that the information in question will not, in any event, be tendered into evidence without having been disclosed to the accused and outlines the

---

[192] A different approach is taken in the ICC Rome Statute, which contains features of both common law and the civil law traditions, while the ECCC further distinguishes itself on this point given its civil law oriented procedure, which provides that disclosure is performed by the co-investigating judges; Klamberg. *supra* note 146 at 274; Tochilovsky, *supra* note 186 at 95. *See* ICTY, ICTR and SCSL Rules 66–68 and MICT Rules 71–73.

procedure to follow when such evidence is introduced at trial;[193] however Rule 107 goes on to provide for a specific procedure to resolve issues that may arise in connection with the use of such information when it is subject to disclosure (namely, with the Specialist Prosecutor applying *ex parte* to the Panel to be relieved of his or her obligation to disclose the initial material, and importantly, showing the information to the Panel).

This is crucial: having access to the information puts the Panel in a position to decide on the appropriateness of the measures proposed, but also to assess the potential impact on the accused's fair trial rights in case the material is not disclosed to the defence.[194] This point is somewhat illustrated indirectly by the *Lubanga* debacle at the ICC, where such a provision is missing. Much of the material collected by the Prosecutor in that case was obtained on the condition of confidentiality; the OTP faced difficulties in securing the consent of the providers of some of the evidence, and less than a month before the established trial start date, information containing potentially exculpatory evidence had still not been disclosed to the defence (nor the chamber).[195] This ultimately led to the Trial Chamber's decision to order an indefinite stay of proceedings,[196] a decision later upheld by the Appeals Chamber, stating that the failure to supply the

---

193   Rule 82 ICC RPE; Rule 70 ICTY and ICTR.
194   Karnavas, *supra* note 129 at 105.
195   Kaoutzanis, *supra* note 185 at 277 ff.
196   ICC, *Prosecutor v. Thomas Lubanga Dyilo*, Trial Chamber I Decision on the consequences of non-disclosure of exculpatory materials covered by Article 54(3)(e) agreements and the application to stay the prosecution of the accused, together with certain other issues raised at the Status Conference on 10 June 2008, 13 June 2008, ICC-01/04-01/06-1401, at ¶ 94 (hereinafter *Lubanga* Non-Disclosure Decision).

defence, or even the Chamber, with the potentially exculpatory evidence precluded the possibility of Lubanga receiving a fair trial.[197]

Also noteworthy is how the rules on protective measures, and in particular Rule 80(4)(e) interact with the disclosure regime, allowing for the possibility that the identity of a witness may never be revealed. In this regard, the KSC RPE go further than the ICC and the *ad hocs*, where disclosure of the identity of witnesses may be delayed, but only so long as the accused is given adequate time for the preparation of their defence.[198]

A number of different protective measures may be ordered for the protection of witnesses and victims (as well as others that are at risk on account of testimony given by witnesses), provided that the measures are consistent with the rights of the accused. Those indicated in Rule 80(4)(e) can only be ordered 'in exceptional circumstances, and subject to any necessary safeguards'. It should also be noted that Rule 140(4)(b) specifies that "a conviction may not be based solely or to a decisive extent on the evidence of witnesses whose identity was not disclosed to the Defence".

In taking these decisions, the judges will have to strike a balance between the protection of victims and witnesses and the accused's right to a fair trial.[199] It is

---

197   Katzman Rachel, "The Non-Disclosure of Confidential Exculpatory Evidence and the Lubanga Proceedings: How the ICC Defense System Affects the Accused's Right to a Fair Trial", *Northwestern Journal of International Human Rights*, Vol. 8, Issue 1, 2009, at 78.

198   ICTY, *Prosecutor v. Vojislav Šešelj*, Appeals Chamber Decision on Vojislav Šešelj's Appeal Against the Trial Chamber's Oral Decision of 7 November 2007, 24 January 2008, IT-03-67-AR73.6, at para. 15; ICTY, *Prosecutor v. Radovan Karadžić*, Trial Chamber Decision on Accused's Sixty -Sixth Disclosure Violation Motion, 8 February 2012, IT-95-5/18-T, at para. 17.

199   Klamberg, *supra* note 146 at 309.

to be seen how judges of the KSC will resolve this tension deciding on individual cases.

Most remarkable is rule 110, regulating sanctions for violations of disclosure obligations; this provision represents a novelty in international criminal procedure, and one that constitutes a significant step towards a greater consideration for human rights and fair trial guarantees. Indeed, the routine occurrence of violations of disclosure obligations, particularly from the prosecution, has been one remarkable flaw in the record of fairness of international criminal tribunals, and one that has been met with the reluctance of chambers to impose any significant sanctions for such violations.[200]

The *ad hoc* tribunals RPE contain a provision according to which "the Pre-Trial Judge or the Trial Chamber may decide *proprio motu*, or at the request of either Party, on sanctions to be imposed on a Party that fails to perform its disclosure obligations";[201] however, as it can be clearly seen, the provision does not specify what kind of measure could be taken, and has indeed been interpreted as leaving discretion to the judges in that regard. In practice, the "sanction approach" has not been the primary option in dealing with non-compliance; rather, chambers

---

200   Heinze, *supra* note 129 at 227 *ff*; Zappalà Salvatore, *Human Rights in International Criminal Proceedings,* Oxford University Press, Oxford, 2003 at 17. See the Final Report of the "Independent Expert Review of the International Criminal Court and the Rome Statute System", issued on 30 September 2020 by the Group of Independent Experts appointed by the ICC Assembly of State Parties (ICC-ASP/18/Res.7), at 152 *ff*, where it is noted that "*Accounts were given of alleged regular violation of the Prosecutor's disclosure obligations (regulated by the Statute and RPE), by seeking to disclose new incriminating evidence after the disclosure deadlines set by Chambers (…)*".
201   Rule 68 bis ICTY RPE, Rule 74 IRMCT.

have on some occasions focused on offering relief to the defence,[202] but overall have reacted rather timidly to the Prosecution's disclosure violations.[203]

At the ICC, where, differently from the KSC, neither the Rome Statute nor the RPE contain an express provision dealing with non-compliance with disclosure obligations, stay of proceedings was in fact ordered in *Lubanga* following the continued non-disclosure of exculpatory information, as recalled above.[204] The Appeals Chamber in that case took a human rights approach to the ICC legal framework to conclude that a Chamber could discontinue proceedings, in exce tional circumstances[205]; however, the threshold to take such a decision is extremely high, as clarified by subsequent ICC case law.[206]

---

202   Fiori, *supra* note 130 at 227. See ICTY, *Prosecutor v. Milomir Stakić*, Appeals Chamber Judgement, 22 March 2006, IT-97-24-A, at para. 192; ICTY, *Prosecutor v. Radislav Krstić*, Appeals Chamber Judgement, 19 April 2004, IT-98-33-A, at para. 187 (hereinafter, *Krstić* Appeal Judgment); ICTR, *Prosecutor v. Augustin Ndindiliyimana et al*, Trial Chamber II Decision on Nzuwonemeye's Urgent Motion for Admission of CN's Statement into Evidence, 20 March 2009, ICTR-00-56-T, at para. 11; ICTR, *Prosecutor v. Augustin Ndindiliyimana et al*, Trial Chamber II Decision on Augustin Bizimungu's Motion for Dislcosure of a Contested Document, 31 August 2009, ICTR-00-56-T, at para. 12; ICTR, *Édouard Karemera & Matthieu Ngirumpatse v. Prosecutor*, Appeals Chamber Judgement, 29 September 2014, ICTR-98-44-A, at paras. 433, 442; ICTR, *Augustin Ndindiliyimana et al v. Prosecutor*, Appeals Chamber Judgement, 11 February 2014, ICTR-000-56-A, at para. 23.
203   Fiori, *supra* note 130 at 229; ICTR, *Justin Mugenzi & Prosper Mugiraneza v. Prosecutor*, Appeals Chamber Judgement, 4 February 2013, ICTR-99-50-A, at para, 63; ICTR, *Prosecutor v. Édouard Karemera et al*, Trial Chamber III Decision on Motion for Partial Reconsideration of the Decision on Joseph Nzirorera's Tenth Notice of Rule 68 Violation, 16 April 2008, ICTR-98-44-T, at para. 17 2158; ICTR, *Prosecutor v. Édouard Karemera et al*, Trial Chamber III Decision on Joseph Nzirorera's Eleventh Notice of Rule 68 Violation and Motion for Stay of Proceedings, 11 September 2008, ICTR-98-44-T, at paras 26-30; ICTR, *Prosecutor v. Édouard Karemera et al*, Trial Chamber III Decision on Joseph Nzirorera's 13th, 14th, and 15th Notices of Rule 68 Violation and Motions for Remedial and Punitive Measures: ZF, Michel Bakuzakundi, and Tharcisse Renzaho, 18 February 2009, ICTR-98-44-T, at para. 31; ICTY, *Prosecutor v. Naser Orić*, Trial Chamber Judgement, 30 June 2006, IT-03-68-T, at para. 77; *Krstić* Appeal Judgment at para. 187; ICTY, *Prosecutor v. Miroslav Bralo*, Appeals Chamber Decision on Motions for Access to *Ex-Parte* Portions of the Record on Appeal and for Disclosure of Mitigating Material, 30 August 2006, IT-95-17-A, at para. 31.
204   *Lubanga* Non-Disclosure Decision, at para. 94.
205   With explicit reference to Article 21(3), the Lubanga Appeals Chamber stated in a now

The importance of clear and strict rules on disclosure should not be understated, particularly when seen through the lens of the principle of equality of arms.[207] Because of the nature of international proceedings and the role of the Prosecutor in gathering information for the investigation, the Prosecutor will inevitably be in possession of valuable information for the Defence's case. Furthermore,

renowned quote "*If no fair trial can be held, the object of the judicial process is frustrated and the process must be stopped. . . where the breaches of the rights of the accused are such as to make it impossible for him/her to make his/her defence within the framework of his rights, no fair trial can take place and the proceedings can be stayed*": ICC, *Prosecutor v. Thomas Lubanga Dyilo*, Appeals Chamber Judgment on the Appeal of Mr. Thomas Lubanga Dyilo against the Decision on the Defence Challenge to the Jurisdiction of the Court pursuant to article 19 (2) (a) of the Statute of 3 October 2006, 14 December 2006, ICC-01/04-01/06-772, at paras. 37-39. See Klamberg, *supra* note 146 at 80. See ICC, *Prosecutor v. Thomas Lubanga Dyilo*, Appeals Chamber Judgment on the Appeal of the Prosecutor Against the Decision of Trial Chamber I of 8 July 2010 entitled "Decision on the Prosecution's Urgent Request for Variation of the Time-Limit to Disclose the Identity of Intermediary 143 or Alternatively to Stay Proceedings Pending Further Consultations with the VWU", 8 October 2010, ICC-01/04-01/06-2582, at para. 55 (hereinafter, *Lubanga* Appeals Judgment on Appeal of Prosecutor); ICC, *Prosecutor v. Abdallah Banda Abakaer Nourain and Saleh Mohammed Jerbo Jamus,* Trial Chamber Decision on the Defence Request for a Temporary Stay of Proceedings, 26 October 2012, ICC-02/05-03/09-410, at para. 78 (hereinafter, *Banda* Stay Decision); ICC, *Prosecutor v. Uhuru Muigai Kenyatta*, Trial Chamber V Decision on Defence Application Pursuant to Article 64(4) and Related Requests, 26 April 2013, ICC-01/09-02/11-728, at para. 77 (hereinafter, *Kenyatta* Decision on Article 64(4) Application); ICC, *Prosecutor v. Thomas Lubanga Dyilo*, Trial Chamber I Decision on the "Defence Application Seeking a Permanent Stay of the Proceedings", 2 March 2011, ICC-01/04-01/06-2690, at paras. 195-99; ICC, *Prosecutor v. Uhuru Muigai Kenyatta*, Trial Chamber V(B) Decision on Defence Application for a Permanent Stay of the Proceedings due to an Abuse of Process, 5 December 2013, ICC-01/09-02/11-868-Red, at para. 101; ICC, *Prosecutor v. Jean-Pierre Bemba Gombo*, Trial Chamber III Decision on "Defence Request for Relief for Abuse of Process", 17 June 2015, ICC-01/05-01/08-3255, at para. 33.

206   *Banda* Stay Decision at para. 78; *Kenyatta* Decision on Article 64(4) Application at para. 77; *Lubanga* Non-Disclosure Decision at para. 91, all *supra* note 196; ICC, *Prosecutor v. Thomas Lubanga Dyilo*, Appeals Chamber Judgment on the Appeal of the Prosecutor against the Decision of Trial Chamber I entitled "Decision on the Consequences of Non-Disclosure of Exculpatory Materials covered by Article 54(3)(e) Agreements and the Application to Stay the Prosecution of the Accused, together with Certain Other Issues Raised at the Status Conference on 10 June 2008", 21 October 2008, ICC-01/04-01/06-1486, at para. 76; *Lubanga* Appeals Judgment on Appeal of Prosecutor, *supra* note 196 at para. 55.

207   ECtHR, *De Haes and Gijsels v. Belgium*, Judgment, 24 February 1997, 19983/92. See also ECtHR, *Ankerl v. Switzerland*, Judgment, 23 October 1996, 17748/91, at para. 38; ECtHR, *Helle v. Finland*, Judgment, 19 December 1997, 20772/92, at para. 53; ECtHR, *Krčmář and Others v. The Czech Republic*, Judgment, 3 March 2000, 35376/97, at para 39. Fiori, *supra* note 121 at 231.

international prosecutors can rely on much greater resources than those available to the defence, and begin the investigations years before the issuance of an indictment, granting them a huge time advantage. As expressed by the PTC I in *Lubanga*, the Prosecution's disclosure obligations are a "key tool in the Court's criminal procedure to ensure the fundamental right of any person to a fair and expeditious trial" and "must be interpreted in a way consistent with, inter alia, the rights of the accused to be informed promptly and in detail of the nature, cause and content of the charges and to have adequate time and facilities to prepare the defence".[208]

The presence of clear and detailed provisions related to disclosure including a provision allowing judges to decide on measures to be taken as a result of non-compliance with disclosure obligations is therefore a positive feature of the RPE.

In sum, the detailed and comprehensive rules on disclosure in the KSC RPE, while modelled against the correspondent rules in other international criminal tribunals, contain some remarkable differences and novelties, which arguably raise the bar of procedural fairness in international criminal law. On the other hand, rules such as those allowing for non-disclosure of identity of witnesses in exceptional circumstances may pose complex fair trial challenges that will have to be resolved by the judges based on the specific circumstances of each case.

---

[208]   Klamberg, *supra* note 146. ICC, *Prosecutor v. Thomas Lubanga Dyilo*, Pre-Trial Chamber I Decision on the Final System of Disclosure and the Establishment of a Timetable, 15 May 2006, ICC-01/04-01/06-102, at 4–5.

6. Dismissal of charges

As soon as the case is ready for trial, the KSC President will assign judges from the Roster in accordance with the Rules on Assignment of Specialist Chambers Judges to a trial Panel, which will include a reserve judge (or a single trial judge).[209]

The trial may begin with opening statements by the Parties and Victims' Counsel, and continues with the presentation of evidence. This is regulated in Rule 127, and provides for evidence for the Specialist Prosecutor to go first, followed by evidence for the Defence and evidence called by the Panel. Specialist Prosecutor evidence in rebuttal and Defence evidence in rejoinder may follow, with leave of the Panel.

Rule 130 contains a provision titled 'dismissal of charges' which addresses the possibility that during the course of trial it appears that the evidence, even if believed, would be insufficient for a conviction, because of gaps in the investigation or for any other reason.[210]

According to Rule 130, immediately after the closing of the Specialist Prosecutor's case the defence may file a motion to dismiss any or all of the charges in the Indictment; the Panel, having heard the Parties (and, where applicable, Victims' Counsel) "may dismiss some or all charges, if there is no evidence capable of supporting a conviction beyond reasonable doubt on the

---

209   Art. 33 KSC Law, Rule 115 KSC RPE.
210   Klamberg, *supra* note 146 at 144.

particular charge in question". The rule does not go in any further detail as to the standard to be applied in making this evaluation. However common law as well as ICL jurisprudence offer some guidance in this respect.

Comparison with other tribunals and fair trial considerations

The KSC rules on the modalities of trial largely resembles those of other international criminal tribunals, with some minor differences. From a fair trial perspective, the most notable rule in this context is arguably Rule 130 on 'dismissal of charges'.

This rule is not exactly a novelty; it substantially crystallises the common law practice, inherited and incorporated by the *ad hocs*,[211] of permitting the defence to file a request for as a request for a judgment of acquittal - or 'no case to answer' (NCTA) motion - at the end of the Prosecution case.[212] At the ICTY, the first NCTA motion was considered by a chamber even before being incorporated in the legal framework of the tribunal, which was praised for demonstrating "great concern for the rights of the accused and, in particular, the presumption of innocence."[213]

Upon a reading of Rule 130, the legal test for a motion for dismissal of charges appears to be the same as that applied at the *ad hocs* for no case to answer motions - whether there is evidence upon which, if accepted, a reasonable

---

211   *See* Rule 98bis ICTY RPE, Rule 98bis ICTR RPE, Rule 98 SCSL RPE.
212   Karnavas, *supra* note 129 at 108.
213   *See* Fairlie Megan, "Defense Issues at the International Criminal Court", *Georgia Journal of International and Comparative Law*, Vol. 47 Issue 3 at at 625, citing Zappalà *supra* note 200 at 91.

tribunal of fact could be satisfied beyond reasonable doubt of the guilt of the accused on the particular charge in question.[214]

As said above, the rule does not provide guidance as to the standard of review to be applied by the Panel in making the determination whether the evidence presented by the Specialist Prosecutor could lead to a conviction.[215] The approach taken at the ICTY and other international(ised) criminal tribunals to rule on such motions has been to evaluate the prosecution evidence presented in its case-in-chief on a *prima facie* basis — taking the evidence at its highest (qualitative) value without questioning its credibility and reliability 'unless incapable of belief'.[216] Judges at the ICC have followed a similar approach to

---

214   ICTY, *Prosecutor v. Radovan Karadžić*, Appeals Chamber Judgement, 11 July 2013, IT-95-5/18-AR98bis.1, at para. 21 (hereinafter, *Karadžić* Appeals Judgment); ICTY, *Prosecutor v. Goran Jelisić*, Appeals Chamber Judgement, 5 July 2001, IT-95-10-A, at para. 37 (hereinafter, *Jelisić* Appeals Judgment); ICC, *Prosecutor v. William Samoei Ruto and Joshua Arap Sang*, Trial Chamber V(a) Decision No. 5 on the Conduct of Trial Proceedings (Principles and Procedure on 'No Case to Answer' Motions), 3 June 2014, ICC-01/09-01/11-1334, at para. 24 (hereinafter, *Ruto* Decision on Conduct of Trial Proceedings); ICTR, *Prosecutor v. Theoneste Bagosora et al*, Trial Chamber I Decision on Motions for Judgement of Acquittal, 2 February 2005, ICTR-98-41-T, at para. 3, 6; ICTR, *Prosecutor v. Pauline Nyiramasuhuko et al*, Trial Chamber II Decision on Defence Motions for Acquittal Under Rule 98*bis*, 16 December 2004, ICTR-98-42-T, at para. 71; ICTR, *Prosecutor v. Jean Mpambara*, Trial Chamber I Decision on the Defence's Motion for Judgement of Acquittal, 21 October 2005, ICTR-2001-65-T, at para. 4; ICTR, *Prosecutor v. Tharcisse Muvunyi*, Trial Chamber II Decision on Tharcisse Muvunyi's Motion for Judgement of Acquittal Pursuant to Rule 98 *bis*, 13 October 2005, ICTR-2000-55A-T, at para. 35; ICTR, *Prosecutor v. André Rwamakuba*, Trial Chamber III Decision on Defence Motion for Judgement of Acquittal, 28 October 2005, ICTR-98-44C-T, at para. 5; ICTR, *Prosecutor v. Augustin Ndindiliyimana et al*, Trial Chamber Decision on Defence Motions for Judgement of Acquittal, 20 March 2007, ICTR-2000-56-T, at para. 6 (hereinafter, *Ndindiliyimana* Acquittal Judgment).
215   Karnavas, *supra* note 128 at 114.
216   *Jelisić* Appeals Judgement, at para. 55; See also ICTR, *Prosecutor v. Ferdinand Nahimana et al*, Trial Chamber I Reasons for Oral Decision of 17 September 2002 on the Motions for Acquittal, 25 September 2002, ICTR-99-52-T, para. 18; *Ndindiliyimana* Acquittal Judgment, at para. 8; *Karadžić* Appeals Judgment at para. 21; ICTY, *Prosecutor v. Ratko Mladić*, Appeals Chamber Decision on Defence Interlocutory Appeal from the Trial Chamber Rule 98 *bis* Decision, 24 July 2014, IT-09-92-AR73.4, at para. 20; *Ruto* Decision on Conduct of Trial Proceedings, *supra* note 105 at para. 33; *see* ICTR RPE Rule 98bis; SCSL RPE Rule 98.

that of the *ad hocs*, including on the standard of review, in *Ruto and Sang*; this was not however done in *Gbagbo & Blè Goudé*, but this appears to be mostly due to the specific circumstances of that case.[217] It remains to be seen how this rule will be interpreted by the KSC in practice.

Considering the largely adversarial structure of the proceedings and the burden of proof placed on the Specialist Prosecutor 'no case to answer' or 'dismissal of charges' motions can be instrumental in enhancing the fairness of international criminal proceedings and safeguarding the presumption of innocence.[218] Therefore, the inclusion of the procedure of dismissal of charges at the end of the Prosecution can be considered a positive feature of the KSC procedural framework seen from the perspective of the rights of the accused.[219]

---

217   *Ruto* Decision on Conduct of Trial Proceedings, *supra* note 105 at para. 24; ICC, *Prosecutor v. Laurent Gbagbo and Charles Blé Goudé*, Trial Chamber I Reasons for oral decision of 15 January 2019 on the *Requête de la Défense de Laurent Gbagbo afin qu'un jugement d'acquittement portant sur toutes les charges soit prononcé en faveur de Laurent Gbagbo et que sa mise en liberté immédiate soit ordonnée*, and Blé Goudé Defence no case to answer motion, Reasons of Judge Geoffrey Henderson, 16 July 2019, para. 8; as explained by Judge Henderson, the *traditional 'no-case to answer test, which instructs Chambers to consider the Prosecutor's evidence at its highest'*, which is *'premised on the assumption that the court will have filtered out evidence that was either irrelevant or lacked any probative value'* beforehand, could not be applied in that case, due to the lack of admissibility rulings on evidence by the Chamber (another key issue in Gbagbo and other cases, which is discussed in page 39 *ff*). see Karnavas, *supra* note 129 at 112.

218   *See* Fairlie *supra* note 213 at 625-626.

219   By contrast, it has been noted with concern that at the ICC, where the legal framework does not include a provision akin to Rule 130 KSC RPE, this legal gap has been interpreted to mean that it is a matter of judicial discretion whether the accused may be allowed to have recourse to this procedure, which has been aptly defined as a "judicial guarantee of the presumption of innocence": Fairlie *supra* note 213 at 625, citing Thaman Stephen, "Spain Returns to Trial by Jury", Hastings International and Comparative Law Review, Vol. 21, No. 241, 1998.

7. Rules on Evidence

The KSC RPE contain a total of four rules dedicated to the admissibility and assessment of evidence.

Rule 137 stipulates that relevant evidence is submitted by the parties - but it may also be ordered by the Panel if considered necessary for the determination of the truth - and that a Panel shall assess freely all evidence submitted in order to determine its admissibility and weight.

Rule 138 then provides that "unless challenged or *proprio motu* excluded, evidence submitted to the Panel shall be admitted if it is relevant, authentic, has probative value and its probative value is not outweighed by its prejudicial effect"; evidence obtained by means of a violation of the Law or the Rules or standards of international human rights law shall be inadmissible, if: (a) the violation casts substantial doubt on the reliability of the evidence; or (b) the admission of the evidence would be antithetical to or would seriously damage the integrity of the proceedings.[220] There is also an absolute exclusionary rule for

---

220   Rule 138 - Admissibility of Evidence

"(1) Unless challenged or proprio motu excluded, evidence submitted to the Panel shall be admitted if it is relevant, authentic, has probative value and its probative value is not outweighed by its prejudicial effect. 2In exceptional circumstances, when the Panel is satisfied that an issue was not known at the time when the evidence was submitted, it shall be raised immediately after it has become known.

(2) Evidence obtained by means of a violation of the Law or the Rules or standards of international human rights law shall be inadmissible if:

(a) the violation casts substantial doubt on the reliability of the evidence; or

(b) the admission of the evidence would be antithetical to or would seriously damage the integrity of the proceedings.

(3) Evidence obtained under torture or any other inhumane or degrading treatment is inadmissible and shall be excluded.

119

evidence obtained under torture or any other inhumane or degrading treatment (Rule 138(3)). Another element is added by the KSC Law that states that the KSC, when deciding on the relevance or admissibility of evidence collected by a State other than Kosovo, shall not rule on the application of another State's national law.[221]

Further provisions contained in the KSC Law relate to the admissibility of evidence collected in criminal proceedings or investigations within the subject matter jurisdiction of the Specialist Chambers prior to its establishment by any national or international agent, including the ICTY, EULEX Kosovo or by the SITF may be admissible, based on a decision by the assigned panel.[222]

Rule 139 deals with the assessment of evidence by a Panel for the purposes of judgment; it simply states that evidence declared inadmissible shall not be considered by the Panel, and that "a Panel shall assess each piece of evidence in light of the entire body of evidence admitted, before it at trial. The Panel shall carry out a holistic evaluation and weighing of all the evidence taken as a whole to establish whether or not the facts at issue have been established."

Rules in this sections that are worth mentioning include Rule 147, 'Questioning of Anonymous Witnesses', which provides for the possibility for the Panel to question a witness in the absence of the Parties and Victims' Counsel, upon request by either of them for risks of harm to the witness or to safeguard

---

(4) A Panel may request verification of the authenticity of evidence obtained out of court, subject to Article 37(5) of the Law."
221   Art. 35(5) KSC Law.
222   Art. 37 KSC Law.

imperative national security interests.[223] Other notable examples are Rules 153 and 155, concerning the possibility to admit in lieu of oral testimony the written statement of a witness, or other documentary evidence, "which goes to proof of a matter other than the acts and conduct of the Accused as charged in the indictment". Written statements and transcripts may additionally be admitted where they go "to proof of the acts and conduct of the Accused as charged in the indictment", at certain conditions.[224]

Comparison with other tribunals and fair trial considerations

The KSC rules on evidence substantially follow the example of nearly all other international criminal tribunals, opting for a system based on the submission of evidence by the parties, the absence of detailed rules regulating the admissibility of evidence, and the free assessment of evidence by the judges.

This evidentiary system, which was first developed at the ICTY and later followed by other subsequent international criminal tribunals, including the ICC,[225] constitutes a blend of common law and civil law rules on procedure and evidence.[226] Indeed, while some common law concepts are incorporated, such as

---

223   If a request in this sense is granted, the parties may be allowed to convey to the witness questions which would not reveal his or her identity; the Panel would transmit the questions to the witness, and subsequently provide the parties with the transcript of the witness's answers, with all the necessary redactions of information that may reveal or threaten to reveal the witness's identity would have been redacted.

224   That the witness is present in court, available for cross-examination and any questioning by the Panel, and that the witness attests that the written statement or transcript accurately reflects his or her declaration and what he or she would say if examined; *see* Rule 154 KSC RPE.

225   Klamberg Mark, 'Article 69 - Evidence', in Klamberg Mark (ed.), *Commentary on the Law of the International Criminal Court*, available at www.cmn-kh.org/clicc, updated 30 April 2017, at 532.

226   Tochilovski, *supra* note 186 at 399.

the preference for witness testimony to be presented orally, in court,[227] the key principles of general admissibility and free evaluation of evidence confer the system a strong continental connotation.[228]

The rationale of not including in the procedural design of international criminal tribunals rules governing the admissibility of evidence, which are a key part of adversarial proceedings, is often found in the fact that such rules exist to prevent erroneous conclusions which might be drawn by a lay jury receiving prejudicial or unreliable evidence; therefore, the reasoning follows, there is no need for them in a forum in which law and fact are determined by the same individual or group of individuals - especially if they are professional judges.[229] Despite this widely held belief, however, the reason for these rules goes beyond the presence of a lay jury.[230] In an adversarial trial, where evidence is presented in a partisan manner, exclusionary rules and the role of the judge are crucial in ensuring that parties do not inundate the case record with vast amounts of evidence of

---

227   Rohan, *supra* note 12 at 101, 102 *"That preference was consistent not only with common law practice but also with provisions in the ICCPR and ECHR requiring that an accused has the right to confront and cross-examine the witnesses against him or her at trial"*, however *"that preference has eroded over the years"*.

228   Fairlie Megan, "The Marriage of Common and Continental Law at the ICTY and its Progeny, Due Process Deficit", *International Criminal Law Review* Vol. 4 Issue 3, at 281; Bassiouni M. Cherif, Introduction to International Criminal Law, BRILL, 2012, at 838. See Piragoff Donald K. and Clarke Paula, "Evidence" in Triffterer and Ambos (eds.), *Commentary on the Rome Statute of the International Criminal Court: Observers' Notes, Article by Article*, Beck *et al.*, 2016, at 1322 discussing the relevant ICC rules on evidence, for which the same considerations apply.

229   Fairlie *supra* note 213 at 281; Klamberg *supra* note 225 at 532; Peter Murphy, "No Free Lunch, No Free Proof: The Indiscriminate Admission of Evidence is a Serious Flaw in International Criminal Trials", *Journal of International Criminal Justice*, Vol. 8, Issue 2, 2010, at 556.

230   *See* Fairlie *supra* note 213 at 257 and at 258: *"it is fair to say that the continental 'free evaluation principle' regarding admissibility of evidence is a product of the totality of the continental criminal process, with the principle of neutrality that governs both the pre-trial investigation and the trial, along with pre-trial access to the case file, playing as significant a role as the absence of a lay jury."*

questionable relevance, reliability, or authenticity.[231] On the other hand, in civil law systems these risks are minimised by the non-partisan information gathering that precedes the trial and the central role of the presiding judge in developing the evidence at trial.[232] This is why the civil law principle of free proof (that all evidence should be admitted in an indiscriminate fashion and assessed for weight later at the point of deliberation) works in continental systems, but substantially translates, when applied in adversarial trials, into a judicial failure to screen material offered as evidence by the parties.[233]

This has led commentators to conclude this hybrid system of evidence constitutes an example of the mixture of common and civil law resulting in a procedure that lacks the due process safeguards present in either system.[234]

Indeed, the ICTY system of evidence has not been free from criticism. In relation to the combined presences of features such as the fact that documents presented by the contesting parties need not be authenticated, the lack of a

---

231   *See* Murphy *supra* note 229 at 552, explaining that *"without this judicial discrimination, the only limits on the quantity and the nature of the 'evidence' with which the court will be bombarded are the limits of the resources of the parties"*. *See* also ICC, Bemba *et al.* Judgment, Separate Opinion of Judge Geoffrey Henderson, at para 45.

232   Fairlie *supra* note 213 at 248-252; see also at 252 *"The important effect that objective truth has upon the evidentiary approach employed in the Continental system is twofold. Because truth plays a seminal role in continental criminal proceedings, proof is amassed by a 'neutral' party in the form of a dossier and then assessed in open court by yet another 'neutral' party, the presiding judge. Procedurally speaking, then, the objective inquiry that follows the impartial investigation obviates the need for 'gatekeeping' with regard to evidence coming before the court. In addition, the system's commitment to truth seeking would find an inconsistent match in 'fixed evidentiary rules [that] might lead to the exclusion of important probative evidence"*, citing Pizzi & Marafioti, "The New Italian Code of Criminal Procedure: The Difficulties of Building an Adversarial Trial System on a Civil Law Foundation", *Yale Journal of International Law* Vol. 17 Issue 1 at 7.

233   Murphy *supra* note 229 at 552.

234   Fairlie *supra* note 213 at 291 and *ff*; for a similar critique on a different issue, the interpretation by judges of the burden of proof, *see* Rohan at 102-106. *See* Bassiouni *supra* note 228 at 792.

prohibition on hearsay, and the fact that evidence obtained by improper means is admissible, provided that it is reliable and its admission would not damage the integrity of the proceedings, it has been observed that the Tribunal's liberal approach 'has led to the admission of more or less any evidence'.[235]

As the KSC procedural framework shares these features, similar concerns may be raised in its regard.[236]

*

All these considerations and the risks inherent to the system of evidence are further exacerbated where the rules regulating the procedure and the timing of rulings on admissibility are unclear.[237] This has been demonstrated by the recent turbulent ICC case law in the *Bemba* and *Gbagbo* cases on the subject. In *Bemba et al.*, three of the defendants had challenged on appeal the Trial

---

235   Fairlie *supra* note 213 at 288.
236   In addition to the similarities outlined above, the KSC RPE also lack a provision prohibiting hearsay evidence, and Rule 138(4) provides that Panel '*may request verification of the authenticity of evidence obtained out of court*', but otherwise does not require it. *See* also the exceptions to the rule contained in Article 37(2) of the KSC Law, which states that "In *principle, all evidence should be produced in the presence of the accused with a view to adversarial argument*", such as rules allowing for the admission of written statement and transcripts (unrelated to the acts of the accused) in *lieu* of oral testimony.
237   *See* Murphy *supra* note 229 at 551 "*There must be an inquiry into admissibility at the time when evidence is offered, either during trial or (which may be more efficient procedurally) pre-trial.*" *and* 552 "*When evidence is admitted it becomes part of the record, increases the overall volume of evidence, and is available for use by the parties in examining witnesses and addressing arguments to the chamber. It not only becomes intertwined with other evidence, but its significance, however spurious, is purportedly confirmed every time it is referred to during trial. It can no longer be viewed in isolation; it becomes part of the totality of the evidence. Rather like cancer cells, pieces of fabricated evidence disguise themselves and gain sustenance by attaching themselves to genuinely probative evidence. Over the course of a trial lasting several months or a year evidential debris has ample opportunity to contaminate genuine and probative evidence in the minds of the judges.*"

Chamber's decision not to rule on any objections to admissibility of evidence raised by parties, and consider relevance, probative value and potential prejudice "as part of the holistic assessment of all evidence submitted when deciding on the guilt or innocence of the accused"; the Appeals Chamber majority (Judge Henderson aside) validated the Trial Chamber's approach,[238] which according to Judge Henderson 'effectively undermines the compromise reached by States Parties in the Rome Statute between common law and civil law systems'.[239]

In this regard, the KSC rules do not distinguish themselves for clarity, where they do not explicitly state that the trial panel shall rule on admissibility immediately after an objection is raised. However, a combined reading of Rule 138(1) and 139(1), together with Article 40 KSC Law, seems to indicate that this is the correct interpretation.[240] This conclusion is further reinforced by the

---

238   ICC, Bemba *et al*. Judgment, paras.. 552 *ff*; *Prosecutor v. Gbagbo and Blé Goudé*, Decision concerning the Prosecutor's submission of documentary evidence on 28 April, 31 July, 15 and 22 December 2017, and 23 March and 21 May 2018, 01 June 2018, and Dissenting Opinion of Judge Geoffrey Henderson. *See* Loiero Chiara, "Admitting mistakes on admitting evidence – It's Not Too Late for the ICC to Get it Right", Amnesty International, *Human Rights in International Justice* blog, 2018, available at https://hrij.amnesty.nl/icc-bemba-et-al-judgment-admitting-mistakes-on-admitting-evidence/ (accessed on 13 September 2020), and Amnesty International's International Justice Team, "Time to Clarify ICC Rules on Admission of Evidence", 2018, available at https://hrij.amnesty.nl/time-to-clarify-icc-rules-admission-evidence/ (accessed on 13 September 2020); Rohan *supra* note 12 at 109 *ff*; Fairlie *supra* note 213 at 624.

239   ICC, Bemba *et al*. Judgment, Separate Opinion of Judge Geoffrey Henderson, para. 38. In *Gbagbo and Blé Goudé*, where the Trial Chamber - Judge Henderson consistently dissenting - employed the same procedure; on one occasion the Trial Chamber recognised 'as submitted and discussed' for the purpose of the judgment 161 items of evidence, despite finding that it did not provide sufficient information to establish their authenticity, and refused to rule on their admissibility, postponing such a ruling to the final judgment; ICC, *Prosecutor v. Gbagbo and Blé Goudé*, Decision concerning the Prosecutor's submission of documentary evidence on 13 June, 14 July, 7 September and 19 September 2016, 9 December 2016. the matter was litigated for 7 months in an interlocutory appeal, with the Appeals Chamber substantially finding that the Trial Chamber was within its discretion in so doing.

240   *See* Rule 138(1) *"Unless challenged or proprio motu excluded, evidence submitted to the Panel shall be admitted if it is relevant, authentic, has probative value and its probative value is not outweighed by its prejudicial effect. 2In exceptional circumstances, when the Panel is satisfied that*

underlying obligation for the KSC to adjudicate in accordance with international human rights law including the European Convention on Human Rights and Fundamental Freedoms and the International Covenant on Civil and Political Rights.[241]

Indeed, the alternative - allowing judges to postpone a rule on any objections to the admission of evidence would have the outcome of leaving defendants in the dark until the end of the trial as to what evidence the Chamber will eventually admit and take into consideration. This denies the accused the ability to make informed decisions as to what evidence to challenge, and what evidence to cross-examine, what evidence to present as part of a defence, and places on them the onerous burden of responding to all evidence submitted, regardless of its relevance or probative value, with an enormous negative impact on the principle of equality of arms.[242]

By their nature, international criminal trials tend to be complex and to generate huge volumes of evidence; in large and highly complex criminal cases, to consider all evidence submitted in a case is plainly impossible.[243] Consequently, the power to reduce the amount of evidence constitutes a very valuable tool available to judges to make the task of assessing the weight of the evidence

---

an issue was not known at the time when the evidence was submitted, it shall be raised immediately after it has become known." and Rule 139(1) "Evidence declared inadmissible shall not be considered by the Panel"; Art. 40(6) KSC Law *"6. Prior to a trial or during the course of a trial, the Trial Panel may, as necessary: (...) h. rule on any other matters, including the admissibility of evidence."*

241   Art. 3(2)(e) KSC Law.
242   *See* Loiero *supra* note 219 and Fairlie, *supra* note 213.
243   McDermott Yvonne, "Strengthening the Evaluation of Evidence in International Criminal Trials", *International Criminal Law Review*, Vol. 17 Issue 4, 2017, at 692.

more practicable - as well as to keep the case record focused on the charges, which in turn allows for a more efficient management of trial proceedings, and a greater respect for the rights of the accused. For all the reasons expressed above, for the trial panel to issue timely and transparent rulings on the admissibility of evidence as the trial proceeds appears to be the solution most consistent with fair trial rights.[244]

---

244   Rohan *supra* note 12 at 111; Schuon Christine, "The Appeals Decision in the ICC's Jean-Pierre Bemba Gombo Case on the Trial Chamber's 'Decision on the Admission into Evidence of Materials Contained in the Prosecution's List of Evidence'", *Leiden Journal of International Law*, Vol. 25 Issue 2, 2012, at 511-520; see ICC, *Prosecutor v. Gbagbo and Blé Goudé*, Decision on the submission and admission of evidence, 29 January 2016, Dissenting Opinion of Judge Henderson; Decision concerning the Prosecutor's submission of documentary evidence on 28 April, 31 July, 15 and 22 December 2017, and 23 March and 21 May 2018, 1 June 2018, Dissenting Opinion of Judge Geoffrey Henderson; ICC, *Prosecutor v. Jean-Pierre Bemba Gombo*, Appeals Chamber Judgment, Separate Opinion of Judge Van den Wyngaert and Judge Morrison, paras. 17, 18.

8. Trial judgment

Pursuant to Rule 158, after the closing of the case, the Panel shall retire to deliberate in camera in order to pronounce a judgment on the charges in the indictment; a finding of guilt shall be reached only if the majority of the Panel is satisfied that guilt has been proved beyond reasonable doubt.

According to one commentator, the position of this rule, in a chapter separate from the 'Trial' section, may be significant in light of the timeframe for the warrant of arrest, and therefore the accused's provisional release during deliberations.[245] At the ICC, the Trial Chamber rejected a request for provisional release pending deliberations relying inter alia on the fact that the relevant provisions 'are all included in the Part of the Statute entitled "The Trial". The defendant argued on appeal that the Trial Chamber had erred in law in finding that a "trial" encompasses the deliberations period and, as a result, that his detention continued to be necessary "to ensure his appearance at trial during deliberations". In upholding the Trial Chamber's decision, the Appeals Chamber confirmed the Trial Chamber's interpretation of trial as encompassing "the entire period of the trial until the final determination of the matter".[246]

Rule 159 states the Trial Judgment shall be pronounced within 90 days of the closing of the case; this is remarkable, as such time limits on judicial decisions

---

245   Heinze *supra* note 128 at 13.
246   ICC, Appeals Chamber Judgment on the appeal of Mr Jean-Pierre Bemba Gombo against the decision of Trial Chamber III of 23 December 2014 entitled 'Decision on "Defence Urgent Motion for Provisional Release"', ICC-01/05-01/08-3249-Red, 20 May 2015, paras. 35-40.

are not usual in RPEs of international criminal tribunals,[247] although they have been advocated for.[248] Notably, time limits are also provided for in relation to other judicial decisions.[249] By comparison, the 2019 edition of the ICC Chamber's Practice Manual recommended deadline for the judgment is 10 months.

---

247   Compare with Rule 142(1) ICC RPE ('within a reasonable period of time'); Rule 98ter(C) ICTY RPE, Rule 88(C) ICTR RPE and Rule 168(B) STL RPE: ('as soon as possible'). *See* Heinze *supra* note 6 at 13.
248   *See* in regard to the ICC Gumpert Benjamin, Nuzban Yulia, "What can be done about the length of proceedings at the ICC?", *EJIL Talk Blog*, available at https://www.ejiltalk.org/part-ii-what-can-be-done-about-the-length-of-proceedings-at-the-icc/ (accessed on September 15 2020); and the Final Report of the "Independent Expert Review of the International Criminal Court and the Rome Statute System", *supra* note 200 at 157 *ff*.
249   *See* Heinze, *supra* note 128 at 18.

9. Status of the acquitted person

Pursuant to Rule 161 KSC RPE, where a detained accused is acquitted, he or she shall immediately be released, unless lawfully detained or serving a sentence, in relation to crimes other than those for which he or she was acquitted. Release shall take place in accordance with Article 41(11) of the Law.

While such a rule may at first sight seem almost unnecessary - as it is difficult to imagine a valid ground for restricting an individual's liberty following a judgment of acquittal and absent other ongoing criminal proceedings, this is not necessarily a given before international criminal courts.

For instance, the ICC legal framework at Art 83(1)(c) allows the Prosecutor to request and the Trial Chamber to subsequently order the continued detention of the acquitted person, pending the appeal on the acquittal decision, 'under exceptional circumstances, and having regard, inter alia, to the concrete risk of flight, the seriousness of the offence charged and the probability of success on appeal". The provision was also on one occasion used to impose conditions on the post-acquittal release of Gbagbo and Blé Goudé.[250] The *ad hoc* tribunals also include a rule allowing the Chamber to order, on application by the Prosecutor, the continued detention of the 'accused' person pending the determination of the appeal.[251]

---

250   Kevin Jon Heller, "The Appeals Chamber Invents Conditional Post-Acquittal Release", available at http://opiniojuris.org/2019/02/03/the-appeals-chamber-invents-conditional-post-acquittal-release/ (accessed on 19 September 2020).
251   *See* Rule 199 ICTY RPE, 123 IRMCT RPE.

Notably, when the KSC judges drafted an identical rule to the same effect in the first version of the RPE, this was strongly rejected by the Constitutional Court in light of the fundamental 'right to liberty in a democratic society, the rule of law and the principles of legal certainty and proportionality'. The Court noted that the Kosovo Constitution does not allow for deprivation of liberty for reasons other than a conviction decision or the necessity to ensure attendance of trial of an accused or their commission of further crimes.[252] It therefore concluded that continued detention of an acquitted person pending the determination of an appeal against their acquittal, in the absence of reasonable suspicion of them having committed a separate criminal act had no basis in law, which made this provision not in compliance with the Constitution.

The result of the constitutional review is a provision that, by not allowing for the possibility of continued detention post acquittal, complies with human rights and the right to liberty in particular; this constitutes another example in which the KSC rules offer a higher level of respect for human rights compared with other international criminal tribunals.

---

252   Judgment on the referral, paras. 194 *ff.*

10. The Ombudsperson

One additional noteworthy feature of the KSC structure is the inclusion in the Registry of an Ombudsperson which may make recommendations to the President of the Specialist Chambers or Specialist Prosecutor's Office under Article 135(3) of the Constitution and may make referrals to the Constitutional Court in accordance with Articles 113(2) and 135(4) of the Constitution and Article 49 of this Law.

In the Kosovo system, regulated by the Constitution, the Ombudsperson "monitors, defends and protects the rights and freedoms of individuals from unlawful or improper acts or failures to act of public authorities." Similarly, the Ombudsperson at the KSC "shall act independently to monitor, defend and protect the fundamental rights and freedoms (…) of persons interacting with the Specialist Chambers and Specialist Prosecutor's Office in accordance with the Law and the Rules".

The Ombudsperson cannot intervene in proceedings before the Specialist Chambers, except in instances of unreasonable delays, but may conduct inquiries into complaints received from any person asserting a violation of their rights. The Ombudsperson may also enter and inspect at any time and without notice the Specialist Chambers' detention facilities to assess the conditions of detention, facilitate mediation and reconciliation in order to resolve a complaint, and make recommendations to the President or Specialist Prosecutor on matters falling within their functions.

The practice of international criminal proceedings clearly shows that infringement of individual rights of the accused - and at times of other individuals - routinely occur at various stages of the procedure; these can go from 'minor' infringement of the rights to privacy in the context of investigative measures,[253] to witnesses that end up being detained for over three years.[254]

Whatever the seriousness of the alleged violation, the inclusion of a forum to hear and to some extent act on complaints of violation of rights is surely appropriate. The lack of appropriate forums or remedies for violations of human rights attributable to or linked to the action of international criminal courts constitutes a serious human rights issue of the system of international criminal justice. In this light, the institution and mandate of the Ombudsperson, albeit with a limited role and no substantial power to impact on proceedings before the KSC, constitutes an encouraging sign towards a greater respect for human rights in the context of international criminal proceedings.

It is also worth mentioning an additional avenue offered by the KSC Law, only after all other remedies provided by the law have been exhausted: any individual, including the accused and victims, is authorised to make referrals to the Specialist Chamber of the Constitutional Court if they believe their rights have been violated by the Specialist Chambers or the SPO.[255]

---

253 *See* by way of example the *Bemba et. al* case discussed above at p. 12 and *ff.*

254 ICC, *Prosecutor v. Katanga*, Trial Chamber Decision on the Request for Release of Witnesses DRC-D02-P-0236, DRC-D02-P-0228 and DRC-D02-P-0350, (ICC-01/04-01/07-3352), 8 February 2013, para. 22. *See* Zeegers, Krit, *International criminal tribunals and human rights law: Adherence and contextualization*, Springer, 2015, at. 92-93.

255 Art. 49(3) KSC Law.

Conclusion

In **Part I** of the present analysis, the author considers that there are a large number of criticisms, destructive and disruptive omens, according to which the KSC is primarily the result of international blackmail imposed on Kosovo in order to achieve sovereignty international recognition and full membership in the Euro-Atlantic organizations.

On the other hand, from the point of view of the author, the KSC will produce some positive impacts on the Kosovar society: first of all, to bring justice to the victims and end the cycle of impunity; consequently, to condemn the perpetrators for crimes that otherwise would remain unpunished; to make moral recognition and material reparation and restitution to the victims, an option that is provided by the 'Law'; thus, to combine retributive and reparative transitional justice process; to eliminate the dominant narrative that only Serbs committed war crimes and to create a multiple narrative about victimhood from the Kosovo conflict, in the name of those who were affected by ethnic or political killings, forced disappearance, sexual violence, ethnic cleansing, torture and inhuman treatment committed also by armed groups whose involvement in war crimes is still a taboo in the collective imagination; to promote accountability, the rule of law in Kosovo and legal clarity; to open a public, societal and political debate on the causes and legacies of the conflict in Kosovo; finally, to contribute to intra-ethnic and inter-ethnic reconciliation and peaceful coexistence.

Some, maintaining the interrelation between transitional justice processes and regime change, sees the Court also as an instrument to change, in a favourable sense, the current political establishment in Kosovo, that would be implicated in corruption and organized crime, where many current political leaders are KLA veterans, who gained legitimacy and electoral support thanks to their armed resistance struggle during the war. However, they also gained popular sponsorship following to their criminalisation as war criminals by the KSC because they are seen just as haunted heroes in the public opinion. According to certain interpretations, the potentiality of the KSC to reverse the current regime could destabilize the country. Moreover, the present thesis dissents from this purely political function of what remains a merely judicial body with pre-eminently legal goals. Every extra-legal objective is an additional *atou* of this new Court.

Another positive impact that could be expected by the Court is the promotion of national justice through domestic prosecutions, which would be seen by the public opinion as a more natural path for incrimination of war criminals. In addition, the Court could be an incentive for other transitional justice initiatives in a more inclusive and comprehensive plan. That could be realized only if there will be the support of government authorities, political parties and particularly civil society actors, that need to engage in promoting truth-telling, normalization of inter-ethnic relations, social conciliatory dialogue, reconciliation and substantial and ultimately peace, not just in a formal sense.

An effective Outreach Program will be essential in facilitating these strategic goals, fighting widespread public misinformation, nationalist counter-narrative, negative perception and diffidence against the KSC, its work and mandate.

Information does not come just from the KSC, but also from the Kosovo national institutions and media. In this sense, an effective relationship should be encouraged between the KSC and the Kosovo institutions and stakeholders, involving also civil society and groups of victims; this could grow ownership from the population. Kosovo's authorities should cooperate with the Court in implementing the 'Law' and providing assistance in investigations and protection of victims. They should monitor the negative influence of local media on the Court's activity, control the possible impact of it on public security, make more efforts in the intra-ethnic and inter-ethnic reconciliation in Kosovo and maintain a good diplomatic dialogue with Serbia, promoting a critical revision of the past.

Indeed, another strategy should be oriented on a more collaborative dialogue between Serbia and Kosovo, also through a mutual legal assistance in the KSC's investigations and in facing up with the problem of missing persons, who are over 1 600. If the problem of missing persons involves also the international community and the capacity to conduct proper investigations, the dialogue between Serbs and Albanians depends exclusively on these two parties and on the effort to find a double-ethnic and unique narrative on what happened during the war and on a reciprocal distributed responsibilities even if of different scale. It is also important to distinguish between war crimes committed during the war and other crimes that occurred aftermath. Serbia, furthermore, should stop using KLA's crimes to counterbalance the crimes committed by Serbs.

Face to the previous debated and controversial results of the ICTY, UNMIK, EULEX and national judicial institutions, the KSC represent the last attempt to make justice for war crimes documented in the 'Marty Report' and a test for

Kosovar society to present itself to the European and international allies as a democratic country respectful of the rule of law. This new Court is also important to enact in Kosovo an inclusive culture of remembrance, where criminal justice is accompanied by truth-telling mechanisms that help in the historical reconstruction of different responsibilities and suffering.

In the last century, the dominant historical interpretation of certain tragic events has pre-eminently focused on the narrative of the winners. Questioning on the crimes against Serbs faces the need for a culture of remembrance more inclusive, developing through multiple points of view and taking into account the diverse parties of the conflict. A different perspective can recognize the suffering of others, building a symbolic bridge linking antagonist parties. A new perspective can avoid the prevalence of a single dominant interpretation. It is important to take into account the voice of all the victims of the war, not just those of one faction because also the minority perspectives need consideration. Multi-memory narratives can contribute to reconciliation. Moreover, memory is a dynamic process, it is no fixed in content, evolves constantly and has multidimensional features that emerge gradually during the time. Maybe the KSC marks a change favourable to a more inclusive culture of remembrance.

Author in **Part I** concludes that Kosovo still needs the intervention of the international community, through incentives or political and financial support, in order to facilitate transitional justice processes and projects, fight anti-EU sentiment, enact domestic reforms and gain international recognition through its European integration and access to membership of international and regional organizations. The establishment of the KSC is only one step in this direction.

In another perspective, the author in **Part II**, starting from a different viewpoint and background, considers that, in the landscape of international criminal law courts and tribunals, each institution has its own historical and political background, as well as institutional arrangements and structure. At the same time, most of them share many common features, and can be considered as belonging to the same, less-than-coherent and still-in-development system of international criminal law, and they were all set out to conduct fair and efficient proceedings. In this regard, rules governing the procedure are of key importance.

In this light, and starting from the premise that the fairness of proceedings is an indispensable requirement of any international criminal tribunals, including the KSC, this contribution has highlighted some notable features in the procedural framework of this newly established institution. In so doing, it has pointed out a number of similarities and differences with the respective legal texts of the ICC and *ad hoc* tribunals, in order to highlight where the rules of the KSC distinguish themselves for their novelty, or increased human rights safeguards, or both.

This exercise, albeit limited in scope, has shown that the emphasis put by the KSC Law on ensuring the highest human rights standard in drafting the rules of procedure and evidence, coupled with their subsequent constitutional review, has resulted in a body of rules that, in several aspects, raises the bar in terms of human rights protection in international criminal proceedings.

This is the case with the rules on investigative measures, which are regulated in detail and provide a certain level of procedural legality and safeguards from abuse of power. Similar considerations can be made in relation to level of detail required from the Prosecutor in the indictment, and the specific obligation to include the provision of a detailed analysis of the evidence as related to the specific charges, which hint towards a greater consideration for the rights of defendants. Equally worthy of remark are the rules on disclosure, and particularly the provision of sanctions for non-disclosure obligations, a matter in which the KSC distinguish themselves from other courts, once again signalling attention for the fairness of the proceedings.

Different considerations apply in regard to the rules of evidence, where the KSC rules follow the model adopted at nearly all other ICL courts, with some minor variations: a civil law inspired 'free proof' system of evidence that has problematic consequences when applied to a primarily adversarial procedural system, and which has caused concerns for the fairness of proceedings. In this regard, particular vigilance will have to be adopted by the judges in applying the rules on evidence, especially in regard to admissibility rulings, to mitigate any such risks, in light of their mandate to adjudicate in accordance with human rights law.

Perhaps somewhere in between these two categories could be placed the rules on detention before and during trial, as well as after acquittal on one hand, and the procedure of dismissal of charges; they both constitute examples of adequate human rights standards applied to international criminal proceedings, but do not go as far setting particularly novel or high standards.

Overall, the KSC RPE constitute a remarkable product of law making, with the potential of representing, on some issues, an example for current and future courts. It has even been suggested that they may represent the procedural backbone of a future European Criminal Court.[256]

As well said before, 'the quality of a criminal court will not be measured by the number of its convictions, but by the fairness of its proceedings'.[257] The same must necessarily be true for the KSC; from this perspective, the procedural framework at their disposal appears to be a suitable starting point.

256   Heinze, *supra* note 128 at 25.
257   Ellis, Mark S., "The Evolution of Defence Counsel Appearing Before the International Criminal Tribunal for the Former Yugoslavia", New England Law Review, Vol. 37, Issue 4, 2003 (quoting Richard J. Goldstone, Address before The Supreme Court of the United States, 1996 CEELI Leadership Award Dinner (2 October 1996)) ("History will judge the Tribunals for the former Yugoslavia and Rwanda on the fairness or unfairness of their proceedings."), cited in ICC, *Prosecutor v. Jean-Pierre Bemba Gombo*, Appeals Chamber Judgement *supra* note 13.

Postface

The Kosovo Specialist Chambers, the last resort for justice in Kosovo? written by Maria Stefania Cataleta and Chiara Loiero offers an interesting introduction into this special internationalized criminal court. The book is divided into two separate parts, each drafted by a different author using her own unique strengths and talents. The first part – written by Ms. Cataleta – broadly discusses the establishment of the KSC. This part is interdisciplinary in nature, since its subject matter relates to the grey area between history, international relations and law. The author addresses a great variety of issues relevant to the KSC that a reader would not necessarily have expected to find in a book of this size. In this way, the first part exceeds the mere scope of an ordinary introduction. The second part – drafted by Ms. Loiero – compares the KSC RPE to their equivalents applicable at other courts. It does so from the perspective of the fundamental right to a fair trial. The author cleverly succeeded to stay focused throughout the second part on a clearly defined subject matter that was sensibly chosen.

Part I – As becomes apparent from the first part, Maria Stefania Cataleta has a particular interest in the historical background of the Kosovo conflict of the late 1990's. For instance, the author boldly defends the NATO-intervention in Kosovo, which she argues was justified – despite the absence of UN Security Council authorization – to end the brutal campaign of terror and violence that the Serbian authorities launched to cleanse Kosovo of its ethnic Albanian population. In this context, reference has been made to specific atrocities, including the massacres that took place in Prekaz (killing 58 members of the Jashari family) and Reçak (killing 45 unarmed civilians).

The historical background is arguably one of the most interesting parts of Ms.

Cataleta's contribution. This section is not just interesting to read, it also contains information that is necessary to understand the broader context in which the alleged crimes that fall within the KSC's mandate supposedly occurred and to comprehend the criticism that the creation of the Court has received. Although the author completed this section before the confirmation of the indictment in the *Thaçi et al.* case, the historical facts included in the book are particularly valuable in view of the SPO's biased portrayal of the Kosovo conflict as provided in this indictment.[1] Maria Stefania Cataleta clearly understands that the suffering of the Kosovo Albanian population should neither to be denied nor diminished, if the KSC wish to gain any local support in order to contribute to the broader goals of international criminal justice.

At the same time, some of the atrocities of the Serbian forces referred to in the first part of the book, have in fact (largely) gone unpunished.[2] As the author rightly observed, many Kosovo Albanians therefore consider the justice delivered by the ICTY to be incomplete. Since the KSC lack jurisdiction to address any of these crimes, the selectiveness of their mandate has been criticized as well. In this respect, the question arises whether the ICTY has prosecuted the criminal offences of the Serbian forces to a sufficient degree to consider the KSC's selective mandate justified.

The first part also pays attention to the organ trafficking allegations. These are of particular importance to the KSC, since the Court's subject matter jurisdiction has been restricted to the Marty Report which investigated the allegations that were

---

1   See Anna Di Lellio, "Opinion: Kosovo Wartime Leaders' Indictment is Inaccurate and Biased", BIRN: 13 November 2020, available at: https://balkaninsight.com/2020/11/13/kosovo-wartime-leaders-indictment-is-inaccurate-and-biased/?fbclid=IwAR3tLCc9CHr--T98_Fmf-TPMnrXJwme9D2ZFu_L2-6Vv_JyK9yDdV2VgE6I, last visited 22 December 2020.

2   See *e.g.* Serbeze Haxhiaj and Milica Stojanovic, "Evidence Reveals Serbian Officers' Role in Kosovo Massacre was Ignored", BIRN, 27 April 2020, available at: https://balkaninsight.com/2020/04/27/massacre-in-meja-evidence-of-serbian-officers-involvement-ignored/, last visited on 22 December 2020..

revealed by the former Chief Prosecutor of the ICTY, Carla Del Ponte, in her memoirs.[3] The author considers the establishment of the KSC both necessary in light of the Special Rapporteur's findings and in the interest of offering justice to the alleged victims of the KLA. However, the veracity of the organ trafficking allegations has not (yet) been substantiated by evidence.[4] In fact, the journalists who initially informed the ICTY of the existence of these allegations, decided against publishing their story for lack of evidence. One of them believed that Del Ponte may have done so out of frustration over the Limaj *et al.* and Haradinaj *et al.* cases in an attempt to spark a new investigation into senior members of the KLA.[5] As a result, the content of these allegations has changed significantly over time.[6] The first indictments filed by the SPO do not even include any charges that relate to the organ trafficking allegations.[7] It is therefore questionable whether the proceedings before the KSC will shed light on the fate of those missing persons believed to be victims of the KLA. As family members have been told repeatedly that their missing relative may have been murdered for the extraction of his or her organs, it is unlikely that the work of the KSC will offer them answers, justice or

3   Article 6 of the Law on the Kosovo Specialist Chambers; Council of Europe Parliamentary Assembly Report by Rapporteur Mr. Dick Marty, "Inhuman treatment of people and illicit trafficking in human organs in Kosovo", Doc. No. 12462, 7 January 2011, ("Marty Report"), para. 1.

4   See *e.g.* Clint Williamson, "Statement by the Chief Prosecutor of the Special Investigative Task Force on investigative findings", 29 July 2014, available at: https://balkaninsight.com/wp-content/uploads/2019/01/Statement_of_the_Chief_Prosecutor_of_the_SITF_EN.pdf, last visited on 22 December 2020, p. 1.

5   See, *e.g.*, Marija Ristic, "Kosovo Organ-Trafficking: How the Claims were Exposed," Belgrade, Balkan Investigative Reporting Network (hereinafter: "BIRN"), 4 September 2015, (hereinafter: "Ristic, "Kosovo Organ-Trafficking: How the Claims were Exposed"") available at: https://balkaninsight.com/2015/09/04/kosovo-organ-trafficking-how-the-claims-were-exposed-09-04-2015-1/, last visited 22 December 2020.

6   See for comparison: Carla Del Ponte and Chuck Sudetic, Madame Prosecutor - Confrontations with Humanity's Worst Criminals and the Culture of Impunity, Other Press, New York: 2009, pp 277-278; 284-285; Marty Report, supra note 4, paras. 149-152 and 160 fn. 45; Clint Williamson, "Statement by the Chief Prosecutor of the Special Investigative Task Force on investigative findings", 29 July 2014, available   at: https://balkaninsight.com/wp-content/uploads/2019/01/Statement_of_the_Chief_Prosecutor_of_the_SITF_EN.pdf, last visited on 22 December 2020, p.1.

7   See KSC, *Prosecutor v. Salih Mustafa*, Case No. KSC-BC-2020-05, Indictment dated 19 June 2020, 2 October 2020; KSC, *Prosecutor v. Hashim Thaçi et al.*, Case No. KSC-BC-2020-06, Further Redacted Indictment, 4 November 2020.

closer. Instead, the organ trafficking allegations may have further increased their pain and suffering.

The first part of the book explains that the international community has "great expectations"[8] of the KSC. For instance, US and EU officials issued a joint statement in which they expressed to be hopeful that the work of the KSC will lead to inter-ethnic reconciliation.[9] The author, on the other hand, tried to temper these expectations and convincingly argued that in order to achieve reconciliation, local support for the KSC is required. Although the Kosovo Albanian community has a particular negative attitude towards the KSC, the author considers criticism at this stage to be premature and believes that popular opinion may change once the population gets the opportunity to better acquaint itself with the KSC and its work. However, in this context it is possible to draw a comparison between the KSC and EULEX Kosovo. This latter court was plagued by multiple scandals, including serious allegations of large scale political interference in war crimes cases that were put forward by the former President of the EULEX Assembly of Judges, Malcolm Simmons.[10] In the absence of an independent and transparent investigation, the risk exists that these allegations will also have a negative impact on the (perceived) independence and impartiality of the KSC.

As the legitimacy of international(ized) criminal courts and tribunals is often called into question, Part I of the book also examines the lawfulness of the manner in which the KSC were set up. In this context, the author refers to the alleged lack of

---

8   Part I of the book is cleverly entitled: "The Kosovo Specialist Chambers, between great expectations and negative auspices."

9   European External Action Service, "Statement of EU Embassies/Offices, EUSR/EU Office and US Embassy in Kosovo on the adoption of constitutional amendment and law on the establishment of the Specialist Chambers", 3 August 2015, available at: https://eeas.europa.eu/archives/delegations/kosovo/press_corner/all_news/news/2015/20150803_en.htm, last visited on 6 January 2021.

10   See e.g. Xhorxhina Bami, "Former EULEX Judge Wants to Reveal 'Wrongdoings' to Kosovo Assembly", BIRN: 25 November 2020, available at: https://balkaninsight.com/2020/11/25/former-eulex-judge-wants-to-reveal-wrongdoings-to-kosovo-assembly/, last visited on 23 December 2020.

political consent as one of the main arguments provided to cast doubt on the validity of the KSC's establishment. In general, she considers local consent not to be a requisite for the legitimacy of international criminal courts or tribunals, given the manner in which – for example – the STL, ICTY and ICTR came into being. In particular, the comparison between the KSC and the STL in this context is an interesting one. With respect to the KSC, the author considers that political consent did exist among the local authorities, since the Kosovo Assembly ratified the Letters of Exchange between the President of Kosovo and the EU High Representative for Foreign Affairs and Security Policy and adopted the constitutional amendments that were necessary for the creation of the KSC by a two-third majority. However, the initial refusal of the Kosovo Assembly to pass the necessary legislation and the subsequent attempts to abolish the Court,[11] the pressure exercised by the European Union and international community on Kosovo to create the Court,[12] and Kosovo's position of dependency on the international community for the protection of its territory, may raise doubt whether and, if so, to what extent Kosovo was free to express its consent to set up the KSC.

Finally, Part I also compares the KSC to other internationalized courts, like the SCSL, the ECCC and the STL. The author focused on the hybrid structure which these courts have in common. Although such a comparison is interesting to make, it is worth noting that the KSC distinguish themselves in one regard from these previous courts, namely: the KSC were preceded by three other international(ized)

---

11   See *e.g.* Petrit Çollaku and Marije Ristic, "Kosovo Postpones Vote on Wartime Crime Court", BIRN: 29 May 2015, available at: https://balkaninsight.com/2015/05/29/kosovo-parliament-postpones-special-court-vote/, last visited on 22 December 2020. Marija Ristic and Die Morina, "Kosovo Lawmakers Try to Scrap New War Court", BIRN: 22 December 2017, available at: https://balkaninsight.com/2017/12/22/kosovo-lawmakers-attempt-to-stop-new-war-court-12-22-2017/, last visited on 23 December 2020.

12   See for example, "Transcript of Interview of U.S. Ambassador for War Crimes Stephen Rapp With Koha Ditore", US Embassy website: 20 April 2015, last visited on 13 September 2016 (no longer available in English), cited in Fatos Bytyci, "West tells Kosovo to create court to hear organ harvesting claims", Reuters France: 21 April 2015, available at: https://fr.reuters.com/article/us-kosovo-court-idUSKBN0NC1L720150421, last visited on 22 December 2020.

criminal courts with jurisdiction over the same events that were responsible for the prosecution of all war crimes cases in Kosovo until June 2018.[13] In this way, the KSC could also be placed in line with the ICTY, UNMIK and EULEX.

Part I of the book, thus, offers an overall impression into those issues that are likely to arise in the proceedings before the KSC and which are therefore most relevant to discuss.

Part II – The second part of the book addresses the Rules of Procedure and Evidence of the KSC and compares these to the rules applicable at other courts. Chiara Loiero wisely chose to focus exclusively on the differences that exist between the KSC RPE and the rules in particular of the ICTY, the ICTR and the ICC – rather than on their similarities. This allowed the author on the one hand to address a broad variety of procedural issues, while at the same time achieve the necessary depth. Despite the seemingly dry subject matter, the second part of the book is written in a vivid manner: Chiara Loiero has a clear way of writing and refers to many problems that emerged from the case-law, in particular of the ICC, making this topic interesting to read. Throughout the second part, the author applied a simple, yet effective structure: First, she briefly explains the KSC rules on issues like pre-trial investigations, arrest and detention, the indictment, disclosure, dismissal of charges, evidence, the trial judgment, the status of an accused after acquittal and the ombudsman. Second, she explains how these rules have evolved over time and with experience from the *ad hoc* tribunals and the ICC to ultimately the KSC. Interestingly, the author considers these changes from the perspective of the fairness of the proceedings – the most fundamental trial right applicable to criminal proceedings. As a result, the second part of the book offers a valuable insight into both the development of international criminal procedure as

---

13   See Council Decision (CFSP) 2018/856 of 8 June 2018 amending Joint Action 2008/124/CFSP on the European Union Rule of Law Mission in Kosovo.

well as the specific rules of procedure and evidence that apply before the KSC. As this part is well documented, it may serve as useful tool to both academics and practitioners who are already familiar with the RPE of the *ad hoc* tribunals and the ICC.

To conclude, we commend the authors for their book, because, in an area of legal literature where titles on the KSC are lacking, the book offers an interesting introduction into the KSC and its rules of procedure and evidence. The time of publication of this book could not have been better, as the SPO only recently launched its first criminal proceedings before the KSC and the Court is about to commence its work. The contributions of Maria Stefania Cataleta and Chiara Loiero, thus, provide an excellent starting point to facilitate further academic debate.

Fabián Raimondo
Associate Professor in Public International Law
Maastricht University

Renée de Geus
Researcher
Maastricht University

Bibliography

Books

– Bassiouni M. Cherif, Introduction to International Criminal Law, BRILL, 2012

– Cataleta Maria Stefania, *Il Tribunale Speciale per il Libano,* Editoriale Scientifica, Napoli, 2014

– Clark Janine Natalya , *International Trials and Reconciliation: Assessing the Impact of the International Criminal Tribunal for the former Yugoslavia*, Routledge, London, 2014

– Clark Janine Natalya , *International Trials and Reconciliation: Assessing the Impact of the International Criminal Tribunal for the former Yugoslavia*, Routledge, London, 2014

– De Meester Karel, The Investigation Phase In International Criminal Procedure, Intersentia, 2015

– Del Ponte Carla/Sudetic Chuck, "Madame Prosecutor: Confrontations with Humanity's Worst Criminals and the Culture of Impunity", Kindle Edition, 2008

– Fletcher Laurel E./Weinstein Harvey M., "A World unto Itself? The Application of Criminal Justice in the Former Yugoslavia", in Stover Eric/Weinstein Harvey M. (eds.), *My Neighbour, My Enemy,* Cambridge University Press, Cambridge, 2004

– Fletcher Laurel E./Weinstein Harvey M., "A World unto Itself? The Application of Criminal Justice in the Former Yugoslavia", in Stover Eric/Weinstein Harvey M. (eds.), *My Neighbour, My Enemy,* Cambridge University Press, Cambridge, 2004

– Focarelli Carlo, *Diritto internazionale*, Wolters Kluwer, Milan, 2020

– Hobbs Harry, "Hybrid Tribunals and the Composition of the Court: In Search of Sociological Legitimacy, in *Chi. J. Int'l L* 16, 2016

– Losi Natale, *Critica del trauma,* Quodlibet Studio, Macerata, 2020

– McDonald Gabrielle Kirk, "Problems, obstacles and achievements of the ICTY", in *Journal of International Criminal Justice,* 2004

– Murphy Coleen, *The Conceptual Foundation of Transitional Justice*, Cambridge University Press, Cambridge, 2017

– Murphy Coleen, *The Conceptual Foundation of Transitional Justice*, Cambridge University Press, Cambridge, 2017

– Perrit Henry H. Jr., *Kosovo Liberation Army : the Inside Story of an Insurgency*, UI Press, Illinois, 2oo8

– Perrit Henry H. Jr., *Kosovo Liberation Army : the Inside Story of an Insurgency*, UI Press, Illinois, 2oo8

– Petrungaro Stefano, *Balcani. Una Storia di Violenza?*, Carocci, Rome, 2012.

– Petrungaro Stefano, *Balcani. Una Storia di Violenza?*, Carocci, Rome, 2012.

– Piragoff Donald K. and Clarke Paula, "Evidence" in Trifffterer and Ambos (eds.), Commentary on the Rome Statute of the International Criminal Court: Observers' Notes, Article by Article, Beck et al., 2016

– Pirjevec Jože, *Le Guerre Jugoslave,* Einaudi, Torino, 2014

– Rohan Colleen, "The Hybrid System of International Criminal Law: A Work in Progress or Just a Noble Experiment?" in Marina Aksenova, Elies van Sliedregt and Stephan Parmentier (eds), *Breaking the Cycle of Mass Atrocities: Criminological and Socio-Legal Approaches in International Criminal Law*, Hart Publishing, Oxford, 2019

– Sapienza Rosario, *Diritto internazionale. Casi e Materiali*, Giappichelli, Torino, 2002

– Serbeze Haxhiaj, *Hague Prosecutors 'Take War Crime Case Files' from Kosovo Veterans'*, Balkan Transitional Justice, Pristina BIRN, September 8, 2020.

– Suboti

– Jelena, "Legitimacy, Scope, and Conflicting Claims on the ICTY", *Journal of Human Rights,* 2014

- Suboti
- Jelena, *Hijacked Justice: Dealing with the Past in the Balkans*, Cornell University Press, New York, 2009
- Suboti
- Jelena, *Hijacked Justice: Dealing with the Past in the Balkans*, Cornell University Press, New York, 2009
- Tochilovsky Vladimir, *Jurisprudence of the International Criminal Courts and the European Court of Human Rights,* Brill | Nijhoff, Leiden
- Zahar Alexander & Sluiter Göran, *International Criminal Law: A Critical Introduction*, Oxford University Press, Oxford, 2008
- Zappalà Salvatore, *Human Rights in International Criminal Proceedings,* Oxford University Press, Oxford, 2003

Articles

- Adjovi Roland, "Introductory Note to the Agreement on the Establishment of the Extraordinary African Chambers within the Senegalese Judicial System between the Government of the Republic of Senegal and the African Union and the Statute of the Chambers", in ILM 52, 2013
- Ambos Kai, "Confidential Investigations (Article 54(3)(E) ICC Statute) vs. Disclosure Obligations: The Lubanga Case and National Law", New Criminal Law Review, Vol. 12, Issue 4, 2009
- Amnesty International's International Justice Team, "Time to Clarify ICC Rules on Admission of Evidence", 2018, available at https://hrij.amnesty.nl/time-to-clarify-icc-rules-admission-evidence/ (accessed on 13 September 2020)
- Birkett Daley J, "Managing Frozen Assets at the International Criminal Court: The Fallout of the Bemba Acquittal", Journal of International Criminal Justice, Vol. 18, Issue 3, 2020

– Caplan Richard, International Diplomacy and the Crisis in Kosovo, in 'International Affairs', vol. 74, n. 4, August 1998

– Cimiotta Emanuele, "The Specialist Chambers and the Specialist Prosecutor's Office in Kosovo", in Journal of International Criminal Justice, 2016

– Ciorciari, John D., and Anne Heindel. "Experiments in International Criminal Justice: Lessons from the Khmer Rouge Tribunal." Michigan Journal of International Law, vol. 35, no. 2, Winter 2014

– Clark Janine Natalya, "International War Crimes Tribunals and the Challenge of Outreach", in International Criminal Law Review, 2009

– Dickinson Laura A., "The Promise of Hybrid Courts", in AJIL 97, 2003

– Donlon Fidelma, "Hybrid Tribunals", in Schabas, William A./Bernaz, Nadia, Routledge Handbook of International Criminal Law, 2011

– Doran Kate, "Provisional Release in International Human Rights Law and International Criminal Law", International Criminal Law Review, Vol. 11, Issue 4, 2011

– Edelenbos Carla, "Human Rights Violations: A Duty to Prosecute?", in Leiden Journal of International Law, 1991

– Fairlie Megan, "Defence Issues at the International Criminal Court", Georgia Journal of International and Comparative Law, Vol. 47 Issue 3

– Fairlie Megan, "The Marriage of Common and Continental Law at the ICTY and its Progeny, Due Process Deficit", International Criminal Law Review Vol. 4 Issue 3

– Fiori Brando Matteo, "Disclosure of information in criminal proceedings: a comparative analysis of national and international criminal procedural systems and human rights law", PhD Thesis, University of Groningen, 2015

– Heinze Alexander, "The Kosovo Specialist Chambers' Rules of Procedure and Evidence: A Diamond Made Under Pressure?", Journal of International Criminal Justice, Vol. 15, Issue 5, 2017

– Heir Aidan, "Lessons Learned? The Kosovo Specialist Chambers' Lack Local Legitimacy and Its Implications", in Human Rights Review, 2019

– Heir Aidan, "NATO's 'Humanitarian Intervention' in Kosovo: Legal Precedent or Aberration?", in Journal of Human Rights 8, 2009

– Holvoet Mathias, Introducing the Special Issue 'Critical Perspectives on the Law and Politics of the Kosovo Specialist Chambers and the Specialist Prosecutor's Office', International Criminal Law Review, 20(1), 2020

– Jain Neha, Conceptualizing Internationalization in Hybrid Criminal Courts", in Singapore Year Book of International Law 12, 2008

– Kaoutzanis Christodoulos, "A Turbulent Adolescence Ahead: The ICC's Insistence on Disclosure in the Lubanga Trial", Washington University Global Studies Law Review, Vol. 12, Issue 2, 2013

– Karnavas Michael G., "The Kosovo Specialist Chambers' Rules of Procedure and Evidence: More of the Same Hybridity with Added Prosecutorial Transparency", International Criminal Law Review, Vol. 20, Issue 1, 2020

– Katzman Rachel, "The Non-Disclosure of Confidential Exculpatory Evidence and the Lubanga Proceedings: How the ICC Defense System Affects the Accused's Right to a Fair Trial", Northwestern Journal of International Human Rights, Vol. 8, Issue 1, 2009

– Kevin Jon Heller, "The Appeals Chamber Invents Conditional Post-Acquittal Release", available at http://opiniojuris.org/2019/02/03/the-appeals-chamber-invents-conditional-post-acquittal-release/ (accessed on 19 September 2020).

– Klamberg Mark, 'Article 69 - Evidence', in Klamberg Mark (ed.), Commentary on the Law of the International Criminal Court, available at www.cmn-kh.org/clicc, updated 30 April 2017.

– Klamberg Mark, Evidence in International Criminal Trials: Confronting Legal Gaps and the Reconstruction of Disputed Events, Brill | Nijhoff, Leiden, 2013

– Loiero Chiara, "Admitting mistakes on admitting evidence – It's Not Too Late for the ICC to Get it Right", Amnesty International, Human Rights in International Justice blog, 2018, available at https://hrij.amnesty.nl/icc-bemba-et-al-judgment-admitting-mistakes-on-admitting-evidence/ (accessed on 13 September 2020)

– McAuliffe Padraig, "Hybrid Tribunals at Ten – How International Criminal Justice's Golden Child became an Orphan", in Journal of International Law and International Relations 7, 2011

– McDermott Yvonne, "Strengthening the Evaluation of Evidence in International Criminal Trials", International Criminal Law Review, Vol. 17 Issue 4, 2017

– McDermott Yvonne, "The Right to a Fair Trial in International Criminal Law", PhD Thesis, National University of Ireland Galway, 2013

– Mertus Julie, "Reconsidering the Legality of Humanitarian Intervention: Lessons from Kosovo", in William & Mary Law Review 41, 2000

– Muharremi Robert, "The Kosovo Specialist Chambers and Specialist Prosecutor's Office", in MaxPlankInstitut für ausländisches öffendisches Recht und Völkerrecht, 2016

– Nouwen Sarah M.H., "'Hybrid Courts' – The Hybrid Category of a New Type of International Crimes Courts", in Utrecht Law Review 2, 2006

– Peter Murphy, "No Free Lunch, No Free Proof: The Indiscriminate Admission of Evidence is a Serious Flaw in International Criminal Trials", Journal of International Criminal Justice, Vol. 8, Issue 2, 2010

– Rearick Daniel J, "Innocent Until Alleged Guilty: Provisional Release in the ICTR", Harvard International Law Review Vol. 44, Issue 2, 2003

– Robinson Darryl, The Other Poisoned Chalice: Unprecedented Evidentiary Standards in the Gbagbo Case?, EJIL: Talk! Blog, 5 November 2019

– Schuon Christine, "The Appeals Decision in the ICC's Jean-Pierre Bemba Gombo Case on the Trial Chamber's 'Decision on the Admission into Evidence of

Materials Contained in the Prosecution's List of Evidence'", Leiden Journal of International Law, Vol. 25 Issue 2, 2012

– Sluiter Goran, "Human Rights in International Criminal Proceedings - The Impact of the Judgment of the Kosovo Specialist Chambers of 26 April 2017", Amsterdam Law School Legal Studies Research Paper No. 2019-23

– Swoboda Sabine, "The ICC Disclosure Regime—A Defence Perspective", Criminal Law Forum, Vol. 19, Issue 3, 2008

– Tochilovsky Vladimir, Special Commentary: International Criminal Justice – Some Flaws and Misperceptions. Criminal Law Forum 22 2011

– Trigloso Andrea, "The Kosovo Specialist Chambers: In Need of Local Legitimacy", in OpinioJuris, 08 June 20, http://www.opiniojuris.org

– Visoka Gëzim, "Arrested Truth: Transitional Justice and the Politics of Remembrance in Kosovo", Journal of Human Rights Practice, Vol. 8, No. 1, 2016

– Visoka Gëzim, Assessing the potential impact of the Kosovo Specialist Court, Impunity Watch, Pax, The Netherland, 2017, at 16, available online: https://www.paxforpeace.nl

– Williams Sarah, "The Specialist Chambers of Kosovo: The Limits of Internationalizations, in Journal of International Criminal Justice 14, 2016

– Williams Sarah, "The Specialist Chambers of Kosovo: The Limits of Internationalization?", Journal of International Criminal Justice, Vol. 14, Issue 1, 2016

– Zeegers, Krit,, International criminal tribunals and human rights law: Adherence and contextualization, Springer, 2015

News articles

– Collaku Petrit/Rustic Marija, 'Kosovo Praised for Approving New War Crimes Court', Balkan Transitional Justice, 4th August 2015,

http://www.balkaninsight.com/en/article/kosovopraisedforestablishmentofthesp
ecialcourt08042015 (accessed May 21, 2020)

– B92, 'Special Court for KLA "cannot be abolished" – Thaci', 1st February, 2018,
https://.b92.net/eng/news/politics.php?yyyy=2018&mm=01&nav_id=103403

– Maupas Stéphanie, 'Le président du Kosovo accusé de crimes contre l'humanité',
Le Monde, 24 July 2020.

– Crosby Alan/Zejneli Amra, 'Explainer: New Hague Tribunal Looks To Avoid
Mistakes of Past Kosovar Prosecutions', Radio Free Europe, 18th January 2019,
https://www.rferl.org/a/explainernewhaguetribunallookstoavoidmistakesofpastk
osovoprosecutions/29718149.html

– Balkan Transitional Justice, Una Hajdar, 'US Warns Kosovo: Approve New War
Court Quickly', 17 April 2015, available online at http://www.balkaninsight.com

– Una Hajdari, 'Kosovo Watchdog Condemns Threat to Journalist', BIRN, 9 July
2015, available at
http://www.balkaninsight.com/en/article/kosovojournalismwatchdogcondemnsv
eteransthreattojournalist

– Gazeta Express, 'Jacobson: Should Kosovo fail, Special Court will be created by
the UN', 3 June 2015, available at
http://www.gazetaexpress.com/en/news/jacobsonshouldkosovofailspecialcourt
willbecreatedbytheun105330/

Other sources

– Eu External Action, 'Statement by High Representative/Vice President Federica
Mogherini after adoption by the Kosovo Assembly of the Law on Specialist
Chambers and Specialist Prosecutor's Office, 3rd August 2015,
https://eeas.europa.eu/headquarters/headquartershomepage/3230/node/3230_nl

– Humanitarian Law Center Kosovo, 'The Kosovo Memory Book', Pristina, 2011, available at http://www.kosovomemorybook.org.org

– Humanitarian Law Center Kosovo, 'War Reparations for Civilian Victims: What Access for Communities?', Pristina, 30 November 2016, available online at http://hlckosovo.org/?wpdmdl=4975

– Orentlicher Diane F., Shrinking the Space for Denial: the impact of ICTY in Serbia, Open Society Justice Initiative, Open Society Institute, New York, 2008

– Heir Aidan, 'Step Towards Justice or Potential Timebomb?', Report Kosovo Specialist Chambers, Balkan Investigative Reporting Network, Robert Bosh Stiftung

– SITF, 'Statement of the Chief Prosecutor of the Special Investigative Task Force', Brussels, 29 July 2014, at. 3, available at http://www.balkaninsight.com/en/file/show/Statement_of_the_ChiefProsecutor_of_the_SITF_EN.pdf

– Report 'Inhuman treatment of people and illicit trafficking in human organs in Kosovo' released on 12 December 2010 by the Special Rapporteur for the CoE's Committee on Legal Affairs and Human Rights. Council of Europe

– Parliamentary Assembly, Committee on Legal Affairs and Human Rights, AS/Jur (2010) 46 of 12 December 2010

– Resolution 1782 (2011) of 25.1.2011 of the Parliamentary Assembly of the Council of Europe, para 1. Council of Europe, Parliamentary Assembly, Report Doc. 12462 7 January 2011, available online at www.assembly.coe.int

– Council of Europe Committee on Legal Affairs and Human Rights, 'Inhuman Treatment of People and Illicit Trafficking of Human Organs in Kosovo', Report No. 12462, 7 January 2011, http://assembly.coe.int/nw/xml/XRef/XrefXML2HTMLen.asp?fileid=12608&lang=en

Printed by
Schaltungsdienst Lange o.H.G., Berlin